State College

at

Framingham

ST. THOMAS AND
EPISTEMOLOGY

THE AQUINAS LECTURES

Published by the Marquette University Press,
Milwaukee 3, Wisconsin

St. Thomas and the Life of Learning (1937) by the
Rev. John F. McCormick, S.J., former professor
of philosophy at Loyola University.

St. Thomas and the Gentiles (1938) by Mortimer J.
Adler, Ph.D., associate professor of the philosophy
of law, University of Chicago.

St. Thomas and the Greeks (1939) by Anton C. Pegis,
Ph.D., associate professor of philosophy, Fordham
University.

The Nature and Functions of Authority (1940) by
Yves Simon, Ph.D., associate professor of philosophy, University of Notre Dame.

St. Thomas and Analogy (1941) by the Rev. Gerald
B. Phelan, Ph.D., president of the Pontifical
Institute of Mediaeval Studies, University of
Toronto.

St. Thomas and the Problem of Evil (1942) by
Jacques Maritain, Ph.D., professor of philosophy,
Institute of Mediaeval Studies, University of
Toronto.

Humanism and Theology (1943) by Werner Jaeger, Ph.D., Litt.D., "university" professor, Harvard University.

The Nature and Origins of Scientism (1944) by the Rev. John Wellmuth, S.J., chairman of the Department of Philosophy, Loyola University.

Cicero in the Courtroom of St. Thomas Aquinas (1945) by E. K. Rand, Ph.D., Litt.D., Ll.D., Pope Professor of Latin, *emeritus,* Harvard University.

St. Thomas and Epistemology (1946) by the Rev. Louis-Marie Régis, O.P., Th.L., Ph.D., director of the Albert the Great Institute of Mediaeval Studies, University of Montreal.

The Aquinas Lecture, 1946

ST. THOMAS AND EPISTEMOLOGY

Under the Auspices of the Aristotelian Society
of Marquette University

BY

LOUIS-MARIE RÉGIS, O.P.

*Director, Institut d'Etudes Médiévales Albert
le Grand, Montreal*

MARQUETTE UNIVERSITY PRESS
MILWAUKEE
1946

Nihil Obstat

Gerard Smith, S.J., censor deputatus
Milwaukiae, die 16 mensis Julii, 1946

Imprimatur

✠ Moyses E. Kiley
Archiepiscopus Milwaukiensis
Milwaukiae, die 22 mensis Julii, 1946

THE AQUINAS LECTURES

The Aristotelian Society of Marquette University each year invites a scholar to speak on the philosophy of St. Thomas Aquinas. These lectures have come to be called the Aquinas Lectures and are customarily delivered on the Sunday nearest March 7, the feast day of the Society's patron saint.

This year, the Society has the pleasure of recording the lecture of the Reverend Louis-Marie Régis, O.P., Th.L., Ph.D. It was given March 24, two weeks after the customary date, to avoid the break between trimesters at the University, during which many students were away.

Father Régis was born Dec. 8, 1903 at Hébertville, Québec, Canada, and received his early education at the Collège Sainte-Anne, Church Point, Nova Scotia, and the Collège de Chicoutimi, Chicoutimi, Québec. In 1926 he was graduated a Bachelor of Arts from the University of Laval. He received his Licentiate in Sacred Theology and in Philosophy at Le Saulchoir, Belgium, in 1933, and in 1935 the

Doctorate in Philosophy from the University of Montreal.

He was professor of philosophy and of the history of Greek philosophy at the philosophical and theological College of the Canadian Dominicans from 1933 to 1942, and Rector of the same institution from 1939 to 1942. Since 1942 he has been director of the Albert the Great Institute of Mediaeval Studies at the University of Montreal. At present, he is also lecturing at the Pontifical Institute of Mediaeval Studies in Toronto.

Among the scholarly works Father Régis has written are *L'Opinion selon Aristote,* a book published simultaneously in 1935 at Ottawa by the Institute of Mediaeval Studies and at Paris by Librairie philosophique J. Vrin; and also four studies published by the Dominican College at Ottawa: *Philosophie de la Nature, abstraction et métaphysique,* (Etudes et Recherches n.1) in *Cahier de Philosophie I,* 1936; *La critique néothomiste est-elle thomiste?* (Etudes et Recherches n.4) in *Cahier de Philosophie II,* 1938; *Philosophie et Sciences expérimentales,* (Les méthodes scientifiques en éducation n.1) in *L'Hygiène mentale et l'Education,* 1940; and *La Philosophie des relations familiales,* (Les méthodes scientifiques en education n.2) in *Les Parents et l'enfant,* 1941.

To these the Aristotelian Society takes pleasure in adding *St. Thomas and Epistemology.*

ACKNOWLEDGMENT

For helping in the final draft of the manuscript and for many salutary suggestions, the author is indebted to the Very Reverend Robert E. Brennan, O.P., of the University of Montreal, and to Dr. Anton C. Pegis, President of the Pontifical Institute of Mediaeval Studies, Toronto.

Louis-Marie Régis, O.P.

St. Thomas and Epistemology

In order to understand the problem before us some preliminary remarks are necessary. These remarks will have the advantage of situating our study within definite limits, and they will enable us to dissipate the ambiguities that seem to be native to epistemology. I may add that these remarks will likewise indicate the essential elements of the present problem as well as the reasons which have dictated the plan I have chosen.[1]

Remark 1

The problem that faces us belongs at one and the same time to the domain of history and to the domain of philosophy. That is why it is an ambivalent problem since it urges us in contrary directions. Thus, in considering the epistemological problem, the human mind is at times led to look upon it as an historical phenomenon and process involving the changes and the stages of the development and progress of the human understanding; at other times, the human mind is led to consider the epistemological problem as a question of pure philosophy free from the conditions of time and place in history. The exclusive cultivation of either the purely speculative or the purely historical approach to the epistemological problem is a falsification of the problem itself, since it remains a fact that philosophical notions are acquired in and through time even when the truths involved are in some sense atemporal and immutable. That is why we must be extremely sensitive to the dual aspect of the epistemological problem, that is to say, to both its philosophical and historical conditions.

Considered philosophically, epistemology obeys the natural law of every sapiential knowledge; it must be a knowledge through the first or highest causes, or to state the same thing in another way, it is the apprehension of order. Now, to see things in and by their first causes, or to apprehend order, is to know a multitude as a unity without the destruction of the multitude; for diversity is just as essential to the existence of order as is the unity which formally constitutes it, and the suppression of either diversity or unity carries with it the elimination of order. From this point of view, epistemology, considered philosophically, arises from the fact that human knowledge is from the beginning and irreducibly many and of many kinds. These knowledges bear with them credentials of objectivity and truth, and yet they seem to be in conflict with one another. The solution of this problem of the multitude of knowledges will consist in explaining the fact of their diversity by means of the cause or causes that account for the multiplicity and the opposition of these knowledges. It is because epistemology gives such an explanation that it has the dignity of being a part of philosophy, for it is thus the apprehension of order in the domain of human knowing.

Considered historically, epistemology is subject to the laws of birth, change, develop-

ment and decay which are the inevitable ac-
companiments of all things human, even the
most spiritual. Epistemology saw the light
of day when the early Greek philosophers
distinguished between sensation and understanding, opinion and truth. It developed rap-
idly thanks to the turmoil produced by the
Sophists and to the philosophical genius of
Plato and Aristotle. Then it took enormous
strides of progress under the impetus of the
demands of the Christian Revelation which
forced European thinkers to probe the nature
of knowing in order to establish a proper
order between reason and faith.[2] But this in-
tensive effort and progress could not endure
indefinitely, nor did it exist without accom-
panying evils; and the great syntheses of the
XIII century were followed by some three
hundred years of metaphysical decadence
during which a nominalistic dialectic pre-
sumed to play the role of supreme judge in
the domain of human knowing. During this
same period of dialectical imperialism, the
physical sciences made great advances thanks

to the invention and the discovery of new methods of investigation, and not only did they achieve their autonomy but they also declared a war to the death against a dialectic playing the role of metaphysics. In this confused and violent struggle between science and a decadent scholasticism, the human understanding was blinded, and skepticism, that disease of the intellect, became the sad lot of mankind. It was then that there began to appear thinkers who undertook to practise medicine upon the human intellect, who set themselves the task of restoring to men the metaphysical health that they had lost. To this end they invented an elixir of infallibility, whose name might change from philosopher to philosopher, but whose substance remained the same. This elixir consisted essentially in making philosophy *scientific,* by forcing it to proceed according to a method which enabled it to control, at all times, the instrument that it was using, namely, human knowledge itself.

From this moment onward, every philosophy which was not preceeded by a critique of knowledge was destined to be considered naive and dogmatic; it was destined to lose its scientific character and sink to the level of the ordinary man's knowledge which could be identified with common sense. Descartes was the inventor of the gadget to control being by knowledge. Kant perfected the invention; so much so, that in his hand it became an instrument of life and death for the various human knowledges, an instrument of life for logic, physics and mathematics, an instrument of everlasting death for all metaphysics which, having fallen from its queenly dignity, became a transcendental illusion.

The scholastic contemporaries of these epistemological discoveries were quite alarmed by them, all the more so as they cast a threatening shadow upon their long established and long since undiscussed positions. But since their anemic philosophy did not have the strength necessary to carry on a fight, the idealistic inventions made far-reaching gains and conquests. It came about therefore that what originally had appeared as a deadly enemy by degrees took on the markings of an ally and a friend. To cap the climax, during the last hundred years we have witnessed the extraordinary spectacle of a widely accepted Thomism which gradually began to stylize itself according to all the fashions and modes of the fathers of idealism.[3] These idealistic embellishments that Thomism received were presumably merely the unfolding of what already was to be found in the very synthesis of the Angelic Doctor himself.[4] Such is, historically considered, the situation of the epistemological problem at the present moment.

Remark 2

The preceding remark had for its purpose to situate our problem in its doctrinal and historical context. The present remark aims to make precise the purpose of our investigation. That purpose does not consist in discovering any epistemological concordism between Idealism and Thomism, nor does it consist in any effort to justify Thomism by means of the methodological requirements of Idealism; it rather consists in seeing sharply and clearly how from the very beginning these two conceptions of knowledge go in opposite directions. Thomism has been pulled for too long by an idealistic tug-boat. It has even been subjected to the dictatorial pull of this tug-boat to such an extent that it is no more than the shadow of its real self, and brings to mind the monstrous picture of a magnificent mediaeval cathedral modernized in a rococo style. To repeat, my intention is not to defend but to attack, not to minimize the differences, but to call attention to the oppositions and to stress the irreconcilability between Thomism and Idealism. Collaboration with a natural enemy is just as criminal philosophically as it is politically. Now it is evidently impossible, in the short time at our disposal, to undertake a detailed investigation of the doctrinal opposition between an idealistic epistemology and that of St. Thomas. All I can do is to point to the fundamental principles. In order to make this doctrinal comparison easier to follow, let us consult the map and see the ground over which we are going to travel.

Our plan is very simple, and is a natural development from the title of the lecture. Thus, when we speak of Saint Thomas and epistemology, we can take these words in two ways: first, the *historical* sense, in which one would show the role which the Angelic Doctor's teaching has played in setting and solving the epistemological problem by modern thinkers; second, the *doctrinal* sense, which would indicate how Saint Thomas himself poses and solves the problem. From either point of view, of course, Saint Thomas must be the center of the discussion. He is at once accuser and accused. One might think of what is to follow in this paper as a kind of court procedure which unfolds itself majestically around the person of Saint Thomas. In this procedure, there will be accusers—Descartes and Kant, the great leaders of idealism, together with those neo-Thomists who have followed their point of view—who will present their own briefs. There will also be an accused—Saint Thomas—who will defend himself and enter a plea of "not guilty." You will be both judge and jury; while my part in the process will be that of narrator and recorder. In accomplishing my task, I shall try as far as possible to hide behind the great historical figures whose positions I am explaining, in order that your judgment may be objective and unbiased by anything that I say.

I

DESCARTES' ACCUSATION

The first adversary and accuser of the thomistic doctrine and its Aristotelian sources is René Descartes, a thinker so well known that it is needless to give any detailed account of his life. Here, in brief, are his grievances against the ancients—weighty grievances, to be sure—which he will explain in his own words:

First of all, I accuse all speculation in the West, from Aristotle to the 17th century (excluding theological thought) of having no scientific standing, of being no more than a systematization of common sense, and of meriting, at best, the name of vulgar or man-of-the-street's philosophy.[5] True philosophy, built on solid foundations and on evidence that cannot be impugned, does not exist as yet, because no one has made the right approach to it by a proper epistemology or by what I prefer to call a proper methodology.[6] And my reasons for making this serious accusation? Well, to give you these reasons is tantamount to giving you the history of my spirit which coincides with the destruction of scholasticism and the birth of true philosophic thought.[7]

"Scholastic philosophy is vulgar or non-scientific..."

When I came into possession of all those knowledges that a well-bred man should have, I was struck by the remarkable opposition that exists between the so-called philosophic truths of the tradition and the truths of mathematics. The former were born of disputes that have persisted down the ages and are still argued.

The latter, by contrast, were admitted from the start and have never been questioned.[8] When I became aware of this fact, I set out at once to discover its cause; and then I made the discovery that the difference between these two sorts of truth resolves itself as follows: That mathematical knowledge has something which philosophic knowledge does not have; that the truths of mathematics are evident, whereas the truths of philosophy are not; and finally, that evidence consists in the clearness and distinction of ideas.[9] I could then conclude that evidence, that is to say, the clearness and distinction of our ideas, is at the bottom of the agreement among minds; that evidence straightway puts an end to all discussion or dispute; and that every time we are faced with the need of discussion or dispute, it is because the idea under analysis is not evident and lacks clearness and distinction.[10]

Moreover, from the fact that an idea is clear and distinct, I remarked that it is also one, and that there is accordingly only one truth in a particular thing; so that anybody who finds out this truth knows as much about the thing as he can know.[11] In gathering together the fruits of this first reflection, which was inspired by the contrast between mathematical and philosophical knowledges, I came to another conclusion: in order to know the truth of a thing, it is enough to perceive it as one, an impossible achievement, of course, without clearness and distinction of ideas and hence without evidence. Whence it follows that there is truth only where there is evidence; and since there is no knowledge except where there is truth, knowledge is unworthy of the name if it be not *evident* knowledge.[12]

Now, the special mark of evidence is its incontestableness or its power of making all minds agree, as we see in the mathematical sciences. Wherever disagreement arises, lack of evidence is always at the root of it. Wherever evidence is absent, truth is also absent and the lack of truth means the lack of knowledge. When we have arrived at this state of affairs we are in the region of probability, of verisimilitude, of conjecture[13]; and this is the sort of thing that the man-of-the-street feeds on. It is also the domain of scholastic philosophy since the latter is shot through and through with disputes and practically every one of its truths, at one time or another, has undergone the assaults of controversy and refutation.[14] That's why I am right in maintaining that scholastic philosophy is vulgar, since it is founded on verisimilitudes and not on evidence. For it is admitted on all sides that all science is certain and evident knowledge. If scholastic philosophy, then, is not built on evidence, it has no certitude and so is not science. Hence the accusation that I made at the outset is just: philosophy, as true scientific knowledge, does not exist as yet since scholastic philosophy is not such a knowledge.

. . . because it lacks methodology."

In my initial accusation, I reproached scholasticism for being only a vulgar philosophy because it was founded without method or a sane epistemology. I have shown that it

was vulgar; and now I want to show why the
cause of this vulgarity lies precisely in its lack
of method.

If evidence is the criterion of truth, if all
philosophy is essentially a knowledge of
truth, then *before* it can be established, it must
have a norm which is absolutely infallible;
that is to say, it must have an evidence which
is at once the measure and the source of all
the other truths which it will discover in due
order.[15]   Now, scholastic philosophy never
made a serious effort to uncover this evidence.
It took its start from sensible perception; and
history proves that all the perceptions of sense
have been subject to doubt and debate, from
the time of Protagoras down to the skeptics
of our own time. These sensible perceptions,
therefore, must be lacking in evidence, since
evidence necessarily gives birth to agreement
among minds. And because they are wanting
in evidence, they are false, since truth is essentially evident. It is not surprising, then, that a
philosophy such as the schoolmen profess
which takes its origin from the perceptions of

sense, should have no solidity and should be a constant source of discord, opening the doors to skepticism.[16]

But what is more surprising still is that the great minds of ancient and mediaeval times should have let themselves in for this mistake—first defining philosophy as a body of certain and evident knowledge and then attempting to base it on a mass of confusions and contradictions. Our astonishment disappears, however, when we begin to examine their logic or method which is not a method of *discovering* but of *arguing* truth. At best, such a method can be good only for the teaching of truths that have already been brought to light.[17] The logic of these philosophers, then, is a process of composition or synthesis when it *ought* to have been a process of analysis—the method of the ancient mathematicians who employed it with extraordinary fruitfulness, and which has enabled me to unify the science of numbers and the science of figures.[18] But since the philosophers of whom I am speaking did not practise this method of analysis, they were unable to discover what I call "first evidence" which is the source of all other evidences that appear to the mind. Moreover, their dialectic methods threw into shadow the only two natural operations of reason: intuition and deduction.[19]

Thus, without knowing it, they became the victims of the prejudices of their childhood[20]; and their extreme haste to admit as evident, truths that were not really so, caused them to create a physic of substances, of substantial forms, and of sensible qualities from which they built up a metaphysic of being as being and a natural theology which was not really a theology at all.

The failure of the schoolmen, then, is the result of their lack of method, that is to say, of an analysis of ideas which makes use of the universal doubt as a means of getting rid of the habit of bad thinking and finally leads us to think properly by bringing us to the only first evidence which cannot be doubted and which even the skeptic is unable to deny: *I think: therefore, I am.*[21]

Let me sum up my case against scholastic philosophy, then, by putting the essential points in the form of an argument:

All philosophy worthy of the name is certain and evident knowledge, that is, knowledge which cannot be questioned since the evidence that supports it shows us the unity and truth of things and compels the assent of all minds. But the story of scholastic philosophy is a story of disagreements among thinkers from Aristotle's day down to our own. Such a philosophy, therefore, cannot be certain and evident knowledge. At best, it is floundering on the margins of the probable and is vulgar or pre-scientific. Its character of probability arises from its lack of analytic method which prevent it from formulating a critique of the perceptions of sense, by subjecting them to the methodical doubt, just as it prevents it from arriving at the first and most fundamental piece of metaphysical evidence: *cogito ergo sum:* which enabled me to construct a metaphysic within everybody's

range and immune to the onslaughts of skepticism.

An "argumentum ad hominem" from St. Thomas

Saint Thomas, of course, has been following the argument of Descartes very carefully.
Now he rises to put an objection: you have
just summed up your grievances against scholastic philosophy, stating that any philosophy
worthy of the name must be certain and evident knowledge, a knowledge which is incontestable since it necessarily brings agreement
among minds. But the three evidences that
make up your metaphysics—self, God, and
the world—have not only been contested but
actually refuted by your own disciples as well
as by your enemies.

First, the names of Locke, De la Mettrie
and Du Marsais are symbols of the very opposite of your human spiritualism. In fact, these
men have made little more than a pure auto-
maton of your so-called "thinking substance."[22]

Second, Spinoza, Leibnitz and Malebranche
have identified your God with the whole uni-

verse and have completely destroyed the notion of causality in the latter.

Third, your evidence for the existence of the physical world has entirely disappeared after Malebranche, Berkeley and Hume subjected it to the laws of your analytical method.[23]

I am forced, therefore, to conclude (a) either your philosophy is not one whit more evident than mine since the whole thing has been controverted and rejected, thus forcing me to think that the science of philosophy does not exist as yet and we shall have to start all over; (b) or, even philosophies that are founded on evidence are still open to discussion and dispute; in which case, your argument against the schoolmen proves nothing since it rests on a fallacious point of departure.

So, take your choice, Monsieur Descartes: (a) either scholastic philosophy has not been touched by your accusations and is truly a philosophy; (b) or it is not a scientific philosophy but merely a series of vulgar conjectures, in which case your own philosophy would be its running mate in the field of conjecture, and metaphysics simply does not exist.

II
KANT'S ACCUSATIONS

The last words of Saint Thomas filled the heart of Descartes with anguish. But at this moment, Emmanuel Kant took the stand and began to speak:

Your last conclusion, Brother Thomas, is good. Metaphysics still waits to be born. Not only has it never existed but it never *will* exist, because it's impossible. My critique of knowledge has proved in most conclusive fashion the impossibility of metaphysics as a science of the real.

The problem of the existence and nature of metaphysical knowledge follows, for me as well as for Descartes, on an established historical fact: that metaphysics has been subject to the whims of every sort of contradiction, swinging back and forth between the extremes of an absolute dogmatism and a thorough-going skepticism. Such, indeed, has been its history for more than twenty centuries.

Pure mathematics, on the contrary, and physics too since Newton, have rallied together the best minds and have made an almost unbelievable progress in explaining the real world; and all this, without the benefit of those everlasting antinomies that appear to be the lot of the metaphysician.[24] How now comes this failure and this success? Descartes tried to make the problem a matter of objective evidence; but the complete checkmating of his system in all its departments shows us that he did not find the real source of truth. For, in reflecting on the problem of knowledge, one thing becomes apparent at once to the mind: that the problem rests between two terms: object and subject; reality and our principles for laying hold of this reality. Now, of these two terms, one was entirely neglected while the other was getting all the attention. "Being" hypnotized the philosophers, while the "knowing subject"—the essential element in the apprehension of being—was left in the shade. The lack of success among my predecessors, then, is accounted for perfectly by their neglect of one of the data of the problem; and it is this datum which I searched out most closely.[25]

My quest was filled with surprises. Whereas the traditional philosophy offered me, as object, stable things, substances, an objective space and time, enduring qualities and quantities, a world filled with objective causality which would make me see God as the first cause of all, the pure sciences, on the other hand, present, as object, only phenomena, systems of spatial and temporal relations which are applied to empirical data that are entirely relative and changeable with the aim of classifying and unifying such data.[26]

So I asked myself: how does it happen that the rigid framework of the pure sciences is able to explain successfully an empirical datum which is by its very nature diversified and contingent? What are the relations of these subjective schemata to the datum of sense? The answer to these questions roused me once and for all from my dogmatic slumbers[27] and showed me the secret of both the success of the pure sciences and the failure of metaphysics. That secret can be reduced to a single word: the notion of *object*.[28]

Object means, not the exterior reality, nor the concept,[29] but the synthesis of the two, and all critique consists in distinguishing in the object, the thing received from the outside, the datum, and what is imposed by our powers of knowledge, their immanent and necessary activity, the concept.[30] If then, by means of an evident and incontestable criterion, I am successful in isolating the characteristics of the datum and those of the concept which is the fruit of the dynamism of my faculties, I shall know exactly what is real and what is subjective in the object; and from this point on there will be no possibility of my confusing the two elements of all knowledge. I shall indeed have critique of human knowledge that will be satisfactory for any field in which it is used.[31]

Having reached this conclusion after several years of research and groping in the dark, I set to work to develop it. The only material that could not be called in question was that of the pure sciences; mathematics and physics. Now, in these sciences it is evident that the datum is supplied to us by sensation and that this datum is empirical and so contingent, changeable and relative. It is also evident that this is the only intuitive datum that we have since intellectual intuition is not proper to man, all our knowledge beginning with the sense even though it does not stop there.[32] Furthermore, if the datum is marked by changeableness—diversity making its entrance within us by sensation—the concept of the pure sciences which contains the datum of sense is marked, by way of contrast, by necessity and unity, as the consciousness of our knowledge shows us. This necessity and this unity cannot arise from the sensible datum; hence it must have only one other source; the subject. So I distinguished these conditions of necessity and unity in the object and I named them *a priori* because they went before the datum, imposing their laws on it and permitting us to grasp it.[33] I then concluded that everything in our knowledge which had these marks of necessity and unity was dependent upon the *a priori* conditions of sensibility and understanding and therefore should never be projected into the real, to become a condition of reality, under penalty of giving us a false purview of that reality. I knew at last when, why, and how scientific knowledge was necessary, although occupying itself entirely with a datum whose existence was changeable, diverse, and contingent.[34]

Only one more step was left: to study the metaphysical concept and to see its relation, if any, to the datum and the *a priori.* Now imagine my astonishment when I found that there neither was nor could be any datum in the metaphysical concept, since such concepts are wholly above the sensible or the empirical; and to have a datum that could fit them, one would have to have the gift of intellectual intuition—a thing we don't enjoy.[35] I could draw just one conclusion: metaphysical concepts are empty, because they cannot receive a datum from an intellectual intuition. Moreover, these metaphysical concepts are the *a priori* law of our pure reason and are therefore absolutely necessary and inevitable.[36] Our notions of substance, of causality, of a Supreme Being, which are central to our metaphysical knowledge, are essentially concepts without content, empty forms: they are transcendent and the source of transcendental illusions.[37] Metaphysics, as a science, then is a Utopia. And this is the final word of the critique which I made with the strictest honesty and scrupulousness: "Lord, let the science of metaphysics rest in peace."

A question by St. Thomas

You allow that substances exist because the phenomenon, which is essentially relative, make them a necessity. You also allow that God and causality exist and that they too are necessary postulates.[38] You say, however, that these three realities—substance, God, causality—are unintelligible because they cannot be rationally explained. But is your own reason capable of explanation? Can you give an account of your *a priori?* Can you explain the unity of a consciousness which is made up essentially of sensibility and understanding? Don't you think that your critique of pure reason is not a critique of pure reason, but a critique of reason measured by physical reality and conditioned by the physics of Newton and the geometry of Euclid? What value does your critique have when confronted with a world conditioned by the relativity of Einstein and atomic physics? Answer these questions and we shall then join the chorus of your requiem for the repose of the soul of metaphysics, as a science.

III

PLEA OF THE NEO-THOMISTS:

With the Neo-Thomists there are friends of St. Thomas who have affectionately reproached him for not having built his philosophy on a critique. These men would like to fill the need of such a critique so that the teaching of their master may not be despised by the Idealists and called childish and naive.[39] Among the Neo-Thomists, some pretend that there can be no metaphysics without the *cogito* of Descartes,[40] others hold that this *cogito* is not enough unless we take it as criticized by Kant.[41] Msgr. Noël, of the Louvain School, is the representative of the Cartesian method. The Dominican Pere Rolland-Gosselin is the representative of Kant's criticism. As for the Jesuit Pere Maréchal, he admits that there is a double critique and that Thomism is a critique in its fashion, although its critique is not a transcendental one[42] and that Thomism does not possess a treatise on epistemology.[43] It makes little difference whether or not one adopts the *cogito* of Descartes or that of Kant, in view of what the Neo-Thomists find fault with in Saint Thomas and how they would round out his synthesis.

"Thomism is not a critique."

According to Msgr. Noël: "The mentality of the Middle Ages was entirely foreign to the idea of a critique . . . One simply never thought of going out every hour to see if the foundations of the building were firmly rooted in the soil. Hence the complete contrast with the *methodic* way of which Descartes was the first to apprehend the real nature and of which we still feel the need today."[44] For, there is no sound metaphysics without critique as an introduction; and Kant, and before him, Descartes, once and for all taught philosophy something that meant a real progress for human thought.[45] It is necessary that the point of departure of an enduring philosophy be a reflection wherein the mind lays hold of itself as an object—a fundamental pathway along which one must pass "semel in vita" at least once in a lifetime.[46] Thought, then, for a systematic philosophy, is not simply *one* possible point of departure among others. To me, it seems that it is the only lawful point of departure[47] . . . and without it philosophy reposes on a postulate[48] or on a realism of common sense which makes it dogmatic or naive.[49] It is certain that the ancients never made the *cogito* the starting point of their philosophy; and if it's only by beginning this way that philosophy is made critical, we must conclude that Thomism is based by its nature on a postulate and the data of common sense and that it is therefore dogmatic and naive.

"Thomism can become a critique."

But if the doctrine of Saint Thomas is not critical, it can *become* such since it has all the elements of a Cartesian critique. It has its *cogito* which the Angelic Doctor calls *reflexio*,[50] it has its universal doubt,[51] and thanks to these two tools, it can manifest the realism of its metaphysics; that is to say, it can justify the substantial realism of the knowledge of common sense which serves as its foundation.[52] To turn Thomism into a critique, one merely has to make it explicit or to recognize the ensemble of epistemological elements that are concealed here and there in the synthesis of Aquinas.[53] Thus when Saint Thomas asks us to reflect on our intellectual achievements and to take stock of the truth that we find within us, he does not think that this reflection must necessarily precede all philosophic certitude. The question would be to know if it is possible and opportune to transport the reflection to which he invites us to the door-steps of philosophy. And the same would be true in the case of the *dubitatio universalis de veritate* of which he speaks at the beginning of metaphysics.[54] Following these lines, we should have an epistemology all built up which would establish once and for all, against Descartes and Kant, the realism of human knowledge.[55] In conclusion, let us say that if Thomism does not have an organized epistemology, this latter is nevertheless there in implicit form; and one can, remaining in line with the thought of the master, make it explicit, thus giving to the "perennial philosophy" those critical foundations which modern thought cannot do without.

IV
PLEA OF ST. THOMAS

At this point Saint Thomas rises to state his case and to plead "not guilty." He gives two proofs of his innocence: (1) first he shows that all the accusations that have been brought against him by Descartes, Kant and the Neo-Thomists are untrue and based on false pieces of identification; (2) second, he gives positive proof of his innocence by establishing the eminently epistemological character of his synthesis.

Proof I

The case which my beloved disciples have made out for my philosophy is a touching one and I know that it is motivated by friendship and by their desire of preventing my doctrines from appearing as naked and forlorn in the midst of the modern philosophic *milieu* which seems so well equipped with critical devices. But the case does not do justice to the intelligence of my followers. For, what is this Thomism which they have made over into a critical philosophy? To me it seems very much like the work of an architect who destroys the house which was built by another and reconstructs it on a different plan. Is it right to say that the second house is the work of the first builder just because the materials that go into it are those of the house which the first builder made? It's still a house, to be sure, but it's not the original house. In the same way, if one reorganizes my doctrinal synthesis on the plan of a Cartesian philosophy, he can call this new thing a philosophic synthesis but it will not be a Thomistic synthesis. Let us not play with words. If it is necessary to destroy Thomism in order to make it critical (even though the resulting synthesis is made up of things that I myself taught), then let us call this freshly born fruit of the brain, a philosophy. Let us, if we are so minded, call it *the* philosophy. But let us not call it Thomistic philosophy. I could not honestly claim what belongs to another.

But is it fair, this attempt at all costs to make me critical in the Cartesian or Kantian meaning of the term? Have Descartes and Kant really made out a case against Thomism? Or is it not something else that they are battling, a phantom created by their profound ignorance of true metaphysics and of the historical texts which have carried this true metaphysics down through the ages? If instead of thinking that Thomism is in danger (a sign of an inferiority complex and a failure to see clearly the inner richness of its teaching), if, instead of being always on the defense, one were to carry the attack to the enemy in order to test out the strength and value of his arms, one would get a real surprise.

How, you ask, can this best be done? The answer is not hard. Descartes and Kant were so eager to defend science, certitude, and evidence precisely because they wanted to overthrow the skepticism which had undermined human thought in their day. To organize their defense, they tried to find a terrain where evidence and certitude exist without doubt. They were looking for the laws of evidence and certitude. Now up to this point we can find no fault with them. But this is not all. Pushed by the desire of truth and the need of necessary or scientific evidence, Descartes denied to vulgar knowledge the title of science, and relegated it to the domain of the probable or of what has a resemblance to truth. Here again we find no fault. Who would think of attributing the properties of science to the knowledge of the man-on-the-street? When we look at Aristotle's logic, we see that it is divided into two parts: the logic of scientific knowledge which is demonstration; and the logic of probable knowledge which is dialectics.[56] Now the dialectical argument starts from common sense as a criterion; whereas demonstration starts from something that is "per se notum" or from a vision of the intrinsic causes of reality. Descartes, then, did nothing more in his method than apply the needs of internal necessity—a necessity that my whole synthesis demands for scientfic knowledge. And when he refused to admit this characteristic of necessity in vulgar knowledge, he was merely making a return to the notion of probability as Aristotle explained it.[57]

So why, beloved desciples, do you go to such pains to establish the validity of the knowledge of common sense? Is it because you would admit with Descartes that Scholastic philosophy and vulgar knowledge are one and the same? Because once you make this admission you will then be obliged to defend common sense against the whole world if you want to keep philosophy a philosophy. For a building is only as strong as its foundations; and if common sense is not made scientific, then it cannot supply the basis for scientific knowledge, much less for philosophic knowledge; but in that case it no longer remains vulgar knowledge but becomes metaphysics. This means that it is impossible for a knowledge to be at one and the same time vulgar and the foundation of a philosophy.[58] It also means that no philosophy can be built on common sense, despite the thousands of pages that have been written to prove otherwise, from the ingenious theories of Reid to the volume of Garrigou-Lagrange on "Common Sense and the Philosophy of Being."[59] Thomism is based on the evidence of being as being which is the proper object of metaphysical knowledge; and so far as I know, I've never taught that being as being and "ens primum cognitum," which is the domain of pre-philosophic knowledge, are one and the same notion.[60] Indeed, if they were not distinct, then the habit of wisdom, for all practical purposes, would be innate, which I do not admit, even though I do admit that understanding, in seizing on *"ens primum cognitum"* in its concrete and sensible existence, is innate after a fashion.[61]

I refuse, therefore, to identify my philosophy with common sense. I also refuse to make common sense the foundation of my philosophy. In doing this, I realize, beloved disciples, that I make entirely useless the epistemology of vulgar knowledge which you reckon to be necessary as an introduction to philosophic thought under penalty of seeing the latter condemned to rest on a postulate and to remain naive. If the knowledge of common sense *has* to be critical, it will be so by a wisdom which takes account of the realistic instinct of this knowledge, of which wisdom will make manifest the part that is true. But this truth, once criticized, will not change its nature. It will still be a pre-scientific truth. The only thing that will change is my vision of the value of this truth. I shall know, in the full meaning of the word "science," that the content of such a truth has no more than a probable value and that it can never be used as the basis of philosophic speculation. The critique of common sense, then, far from making it a suitable foundation of philosophy, can only widen the breach that separates the two forms of knowledge. All the accusations of Descartes, all the fears of my disciples, are rooted in the erroneous belief: that my philosophy is identical with vulgar knowledge. I refuse to admit this identification; and so all their proofs prove nothing. They have attacked and defended a pseudo-Thomism![62]

Proof II

I shall now sketch out briefly the major lines of a true Thomistic epistemology—an epistemology which is not merely implicit but whose existence is complete and workable for anyone who takes the trouble to probe to the bottom of my philosophy, who has no idealistic prejudices, and who is not too much preoccupied with the problem of historical concordances. This *exposé,* short and to the point, will show you at once the strength of my doctrines and the weakness of the so-called idealistic critique.

Position of the Epistemological Problem

Everybody agrees in making the epistemological problem a problem of philosophy, whether one places it at the start, in the middle or at the end.[63] Now the major, or should I say, the unique problem of philosophy is the existence of "the many"; and the whole story of philosophic speculation is one long and continuous effort of the human intelligence to explain this fact which is so repugnant to our reason. For, "the many," as such, is unintelligible, a huge disorder, a profound irrationality. Philosophy is simply an effort to reduce "the many" to "one," to get rid of disorder and replace it with order: whence that penetrating description of the philosopher, given by Aristotle: "It is the part of the wise man to set things in order.[63] Why are Parmenides, Heraclitus, the Greek cosmologists, Plato, Aristotle, all called philosophers? Because they tried to reconcile unity and multiplicity in both the real and our knowledge of the real. We call metaphysics that part of philosophy which unifies the masses upon masses of beings by the oneness of their cause. In the same way, we call epistemology that part of philosophy which reconciles the multitude of our knowledges, binding them together in a unity.

The epistemological problem, therefore, concerns itself essentially with the opposition that exists between several knowledges, and the science of epistemology is the solution of this problem—or the *attempt* to solve it. Now the destroying of this opposition of knowledges can be accomplished in two ways: (1) first, by denying that there is any multiplicity; in which case, knowledge is explained by reference to a single univocal type of evidence and truth, and everything that is not measured by this model is cast out from the domain of knowledge as error, or verisimilitude, or conjecture, and not true knowledge; (2) second, by reconciling unity with multiplicity, by accepting all cognitive experience; in which case several different types of knowledge are admitted as opposed to one another but a higher and superior knowledge is created in order to bring unity out of diversity.

The first of these two courses would give rise to epistemological monism, the second to epistemological pluralism.

There is, however, a third hypothesis which might be advanced; that our knowledges are multiple but that they are juxtaposed, one with another, without any unification. Here we have two widely differing groups of men to deal with: a) The skeptics, who have attempted a unification but haven't succeeded in achieving one and who admit the antinomies, all the while deploring them.

This, of course, is no epistemology. b) The general run of mankind who, without any reflection, and either on the evidence of their senses or on the credence they give to the pronouncement of the scientists and the philosophers, admit truths that are obviously contradictory without their being aware of such contradictions. This is merely vulgar knowledge, and also no epistemology.

The existence of a multitude of knowledge which present themselves as true and yet opposed to each other—such is the epistemological problem at its roots, a fact immanent and conscious, of which every man who reflects can be aware.[64] This fact, moreover, is the starting point of many other questions or problems of an epistemological nature, all of which we can sum up in the following manner: (1) are the knowledges that present themselves as true, really true? (2) if they are true, how is this multitude of truths to be explained? (3) if they are multiple, how is their multiplicity to be reduced to unity? Such are the three great epistemological problems which have posed themselves since the start of philosophic speculation. Their solution is the proper subject matter of epistemology as I conceive it.

Solution of the Epistemological Problem:
"Truth is really multiple."

If you were to ask Descartes and Kant: is there a multiplicity of immediate truths of a disparate nature, that is to say, truths whose content is not comparable, they would reply with one voice: no! And if you object that *your* experience and *theirs* and that of the whole human race presents this multiplicity to consciousness, they would say: its an illusion; an illusion of the senses for Descartes whose epistemology rests upon an *intellectual* intuition; an illusion of intelligence for Kant whose epistemology rests on a *sensible* intuition.[65] The role of epistemology is precisely to put us on our guard against such an illusion and make us admit the truth only where it is found. But where *is* it found? The Cartesian epistemology says: in your search for truth don't trust the senses because they are essentially deceitful and you can't rely on them. The Kantian epistemology says: don't trust your reason because it is essentially deceitful, furnishing you with concepts without content and so without truth. The net result of the epistemology of Descartes and Kant is this: neither man explains the multiplicity of truths of which the human mind is conscious. On the contrary each explains such multiplicity as an illusion, the one, of the senses; the other, of reason. Their epistemology is monistic.

But a monistic epistemology cannot be philosophic! For we have just seen that philosophy is by its nature a vision of order and that order implies multiplicity since it is the form of the latter,[66] the relation of one thing to another. Take away "the many" and you have nothing to set in order and so neither a problem nor a solution. But if a monistic epistemology cannot be philosophic, it is necessarily "scientific" in the strict meaning of this term, that is to say, it does not start from all the evidences in building itself up, but only from one, such as that which characterizes a science chosen as *the* science. For, scientific evidence, by its very definition, is unique, that is, it is always realized according to the same type or schema, a type or schema which excludes all other types of evidence since every science is characterized by its formal object and since every formal object of a habit excludes the formal objects of other habits.[67] But to do this is to reduce the formal object of a power to that of a habit, thereby making a habit of the power, which is just what Descartes did,[68] or to make of the power, not a principle of knowledge, but an *a priori* form of a matter to be known, which is exactly what Kant did.[69]

If, then, the idealistic epistemologies have discovered only one type of truth because their point of departure, instead of being the ensemble of several human evidences, was merely one particular evidence which they set up as the rule of *all* evidence; if, moreover, the point of departure of an epistemology is the fact of human knowledge in all its integrity, then let us start from this fact: that there exists in human consciousness, truths of all sorts, immediate and mediate, intellectual and sensible, universal and particular; and since no one has yet proved that these truths are illusions without avowing that such illusions are natural and inevitable, let us try to show their reality and to explain their multiplicity.

"A multitude of truths is possible."

The very errors to which Idealism has given rise, teach us a lesson: the first and last word of any epistemology is not of an epistemological order but is pronounced by metaphysics or by a pseudo-metaphysics. Let us look at the nature of truth. It is essentially an accord between that which is known and that which is.[70] This means that it is a relation. More specifically, it is a relation of measure and thing measured, the act of knowledge being the thing measured and the reality the measure. In a relation of this sort, the measure is the formal element; the thing measured is the material element. Both together constitute the whole of the relation and without each other are unintelligible;[71] so much so that if you change the measure element you change the relation. Now what are the elements in the present case? They are: reality, on the one side; and human knowledge, on the other, the latter being measured by the former.

The point of departure of every epistemology, therefore, will be the acceptance of a measure of knowledge, that is to say, a certain conception of reality.[72] If reality is conceived as being one, then all knowledges will be necessarily measured by this unity. If, on the other hand, reality is conceived as diverse or multiple, then the measures will be multiple and there is the possibility of several diverse knowledges. Now, in Idealism, it is a pseudo-metaphysics which defines the measure or the reality. Moreover, it is either mathematics or physics which plays this role; and since each is a particular science, then Idealism excludes the diversity of the real. Its epistemology, having such a point of departure, can come to nothing except unity. But if it is metaphysics which gives to epistemology its point of departure or its measure of knowledge, then, since this measure is diversity,[73] epistemology can arrive at a plurality of truths. That is why I said a moment ago that the first word of any epistemology is uttered by metaphysics or by a pseudo-metaphysics.

But it is not only the point of departure of an epistemology which comes from metaphysics; its point of arrival is also from the same source. This point of arrival is the knowing subject, since it is the subject that is measured by being; and since it is a question of explaining the manifoldness of truth, if the diversity of measures makes this manifoldness *possible,* then the diversity of things measured, actualizes this possibility, explains it, takes account of it in a definite way. Here let us go back to Idealism to illustrate the point. Why did Descartes admit only intellectual knowledge? Because man is spirit, because reason is the only power of knowledge *measurable* by the real. Hence all his ideas are intellectual, and include the passions, the sufferings, the images, and so on, that are caused by the body.

Kant, on the other hand, admitted the subjective possibility of a multitude of truths because he distinguished between reason and sensibility, in such wise that if there were a possibility of reason's entering in contact with an intelligible measure, there would be metaphysical truths.

To explain, therefore, the multitude of human truths, it is necessary not only that the measure be diverse but that the things measured be different too. In other words, it is necessary that there be multiple principles and multiple acts of knowledge. Now what science will explain for us the possibility of a multitude of principles and acts of knowledge? Metaphysics, of course, when it defines man.[74] Metaphysics, then, has the last word to say in any epistemology. It is the alpha and omega of epistemological science.

Now let us compare the pseudo-metaphysical conception of man with the truly metaphysical notion of him. Cartesian idealism makes him a thinking substance, with a body thrown in as a kind of useless appendage.

Kantian idealism makes him a pure reason chained by sensibility, which it informs without knowing the why, or how, and of which it is, in truth, a prisoner. Real metaphysics, by contrast, sees in man a creature, therefore, a being essentially directed towards an end by his Creator Who is at the same time the source and perfection of everything he is.[75] Placed on the confines of two orders, he is related to spirits and to bodies without being one or the other exclusively. He is a substantial composite of flesh and spirit, a hylomorphic creature, which means that his oneness is not the oneness of simplicity but of composition. Now, every created nature is predestined to an end since it is by nature made up of being and non-being; and every nature that is plunged in time is a reality on the road to a perfection which it will attain only by degrees.[76] To reach the goal of excellence which was set up for it by another, created natures make use of movements that come from themselves as secondary causes, but which have been given to them by the first cause precisely so that they may attain the destiny for which they were made. A movement of this kind is called natural; and in substances capable of knowing, it is called knowledge.[77] Further, the word "immanent" is used to designate such movements of knowledge and in this way they are distinguished from purely physical movements.

For, *operatio sequitur esse.*[78] This metaphysical law of causality is the key to the knowledge which the subject produces. If the knowing subject is a hylomorphic substance, the operation which springs from it will also be hylomorphic; and the term of this operation, its measure, will be hylomorphic in the same way, so that human knowledge will be multiform by its very nature and the epistemology which explains this knowledge will be by its very nature pluralistic.[79]

The plurality of truth, point of departure of all philosophic epistemology, is made possible and understandable, then, only when metaphysics has defined being as multiform and man as possessing a diversity of cognitive principles. What, then, is the center of an epistemological study of this multitude? It is the notion of *object,* and we must thank Kant for having stressed the importance of this notion and for having made it the central part of all epistemology.[80] The object is not external reality taken in the absolute, but external reality in so far as it bears a relation to the knowing subject, in so far as it exists in the soul.[81] For since the soul is endowed with sensibility and intelligence, it has two possible existences of things in it, two objects of knowledge specifically distinct: sensible objects and intelligible objects; whence arises the two major categories of truth: sensible truths which are essentially contingent and changeable; and intelligible truths which are necessary and unchangeable. The confusion of these two kinds of truth leads to skepticism; the denial of one or the other leads to idealism; but the acceptance of both, while their distinction is still maintained, is the very essence of the Thomistic epistemology, its basic realism, and the only realism that truthfully takes

account of the complexity of human knowledge.[82]

"A multitude of truths can be unified."

A philosophic epistemology ought to begin
with the fact of the plurality of truths and explain this plurality. But above all, it ought to
set in order and unify these diverse truths
since it is proper to philosophic knowledge to
reconcile unity and multiplicity.[83] Now how
does philosophy unify the many? By
causality,[84] to be sure! This it is that explains
how the two definitions of philosophy—one,
by order, the other as knowledge of things in
their causes—are just two expressions of the
same reality: philosophic knowledge. There
are four causes to which all diverse truths are
related and by which they are unified:

1. The material cause is intelligence, the
only possible *subject* of true knowledge[85] since
truth, with its demands of duality and of synthesis, can be found only in the judgment of
the intellectual power. Intelligence, therefore,
is the sole reservoir of all our truths, whatever
be their nature.

2. The formal cause is being, the total object of our knowledge. All that we know as true, whether it be sensible or intelligible, we know as being.[86] For the object of a power and of its activity, is precisely the form of the object.[87] This form is analogical, it embraces realities utterly diverse, such as first matter and God, as it mounts on the ladder of being whose rungs are the ascendant gradients of reality. All this is the very life of intelligence as it apprehends things under the aspect of being. There, indeed, is the mystery of knowledge which rationalism cannot explain and of which only the intuition that characterizes every intelligence can give a satisfactory account.[88]

3. The efficient cause is man. And by "man" I mean not the soul alone nor any single power which causes knowledge and makes us conscious of truth, but man whole and entire, his body and his soul. For it is only *man* who exists and is the subject of his actions, according to the dictum: "actiones sunt suppositorum."[89] To hypostasize the powers

of man is to make the unity of diverse truths unintelligible, since each of our cognitive powers—sensible as well as intellectual—has its role to perform and its contribution to make; and only the ensemble of *all* our powers can give an account of truth in all its fullness.[90] Only this continual co-operation of diverse powers of knowledge with diverse functions to perform, brought together in the unity of a substantial subject, which is the unique source of all these multiform activities—only this co-operation, to repeat, can explain the actual unity of the multitude of truths that we know.

4. The final cause is what we may call, without irreverence, a divine mimicry, a kind of sharing in the infinite perfection of God[91] by adding to our own being all the excellences that we find in beings outside of ourselves. Everything that is, is the realization of a divine idea and possesses an ontological truth. And formal truth consists in the immanent enjoyment of all these divine ideas which God has projected into the world, and thus in a

gradual building up of our being which makes us draw closer and closer to our divine model. Using these truths as the rungs on the ladder of being, we shall ascend slowly toward beatific truth whose possession will be our eternal happiness. And it is here that wisdom intervenes to make a hierarchy of all the truths that man possesses, to distinguish between the fallible and infallible sources of truth,[92] to judge of the richness of the evidence and certitude of each truth,[93] to join the proper object of human intelligence, which is material being, to its final object which is God.

Such is the unity of a real science of epistemology which starts with the unity of the source of all human operations and explains them, in the end, by the final unity of all truths, however diverse, in the oneness of God Who is possessed by intelligence as *the* truth.

CONCLUSION

At the beginning of his Metaphysics[94] Aristotle explains the social character of the acquisition of truth and says: "It is just that we should be grateful not only to those with whose views we may agree, but also to those who have expressed more superficial views; for those also contributed something, by developing, before us, the powers of thought." And Saint Thomas adds: "These men who disagreed with each other compel us to discuss things more strictly and to seek for a more limpid vision of truth."[95] I am sure that the idealist epistemologies have done a great deal to attract the attention of philosophers to the particular difficulty that the knowledge-problem presents. They have forced us to re-read texts of the Angelic Doctor more carefully in order to discover the wonderful synthesis that it contains. But I feel I haven't done justice in this lecture either to the Idealists and Neo-Thomists, on the one hand, or to Saint Thomas, on the other.

But if you leave here with the idea that the epistemological problem is one of the hardest in all philosophy, if you go away with the intent of searching further into this problem and of trying to get a clear picture of it, my work won't be without fruit and I shall be satisfied. But most of all, I shall be happy if you carry away with you the conviction that only the philosophy of Saint Thomas has the principles for the solution of the problem, that his philosophy has nothing to borrow from the Idealist epistemologies, that it has, in fact, the remedy for all the errors that flow from those epistemologies. For then, you will agree that Saint Thomas' philosophy is *the* philosophy, that it possesses the vitality which, as Mr. Gilson humorously puts it, "buries all its undertakers." The doctrines of Descartes and Kant have passed away, the teaching of the Angelic Doctor remains. I hope it will be, for all of us, not merely an ancient text with an historical value, but a reality and a part of the very life of our minds.

NOTES

1.   A complete bibliography on the subject of this
lecture would constitute a whole volume by itself.
I shall therefore be content to mention only those
works that I have actually used in the course of
this study. For the many works in epistemology
which have appeared in the last hundred years,
the reader can consult the two following bibliog-
raphies: Mandonnet et Destrez, *Bibliographie
thomiste* (Le Saulchoir, Kain, 1921) nn. 796-875;
Bourke, V. J., *Thomistic Bibliography* (The Modern Schoolman, St. Louis, 1945,) nn. 2216-2741.

Principal works used in the preparation of this
lecture:

a) Dictionaries and lexicons: cf. Schütz, L.,
Thomas Lexicon, 2 Aufl., (Paderborn, 1895);
Baldwin, J. M., *Dictionary of Philosophy and
Psychology,* (New York, 1901) 3 vols; Eisler,
R., *Wörterbuch der Philosophischen Begriffe,*
(Berlin, 1927-1930) 3 vols.

b) Texts of the authors studied: cf. Sancti Thomas
Aquinatis *Opera omnia,* (Parmae, 1852-1873) 25
vols; Descartes, R., *Oeuvres complètes,* (Adam-
Tannery, Paris, 1897-1913) 13 vols; Kant, E.,
Kants gesmmalte Schriften, (Berlin, 1910-1914)
4 vols. [For practical purposes, the references in
this lecture are given to the English translation of
the *Critique of Pure Reason,* by Norman Kemp
Smith, (Macmillan, London, 1902)]; Noël, Msgr.
L., *Notes d'Epistémologie thomiste,* (Louvain,
1925); *Le Réalisme immédiat,* (Louvain, 1938);
Maréchal, J., *Le point de départ de la métaphysique,* Cahier V.: *Le Thomisme devant la*

philosophie critique (Louvain, 1926) ; Roland-Gosselin, M.D., *Essai d'une étude critique de la connaissance,* (Paris, Vrin, 1932) ; Picard, G., *Le problème critique fondamental* (Archives de Philosophie, vol. I, Cahier II, Paris, Beauchesne, 1932).

c) Studies on the possibility or the impossibility of a critique in Thomism: cf. Gilson, E., *Le Réalisme méthodique,* (Paris, Tequi, 1935) ; *Réalisme thomiste et critique de la connaissance,* (Paris, Vrin, 1939) ; Régis, L. M., *La critique néo-Thomiste est-elle Thomiste? Etudes et Re-cherches,* Philosophie, Cahier II (Ottawa, 1938) pp. 93-199; Jolivet R., *Le Thomisme et la critique de la connaissance,* (Paris, Desclée de Brou-wer, 1933) ; Garrigou-Lagrange, R., *Le sens com-mun, la philosophie de l'Etre et les formules dogmatiques* (Paris, Desclee De Brouwer, 1927) ; *Le Réalisme du principe de Finalité,* (Paris,, Desclee De Brower, 1932), especially pp. 148-260; Maritain, J. *Les Degrés du Savoir,* (Paris, Desclée De Brouwer, 1932) especially pp. 137-263; Smith, G., "A Date in the History of Epistemology," *The Thomist,* (New York, Sheed and Ward, V, 1943), 246-255.

2. There is very little agreement among philos-ophers on the terminology of epistemology or even on its meaning. The *De opinione et de veritate* of the ancient Physicists contains the beginnings of a theory of knowledge. Plato dealt with the nature of knowledge in such dialogues as the *Thaetetus;* while in Aristotle, epistemological notions may be

found here and there in the *De Anima*, the *Metaphysics* and the *Posterior Analytics*. So too, elements of an epistemology can be found in the Greek commentators of Plato and Aristotle. In the middle ages it is in commentaries on the *Isagoge* of Porphyry, in countless *Tractatus logicae, Summae de dialectica, Compendia logicae, Quodlibeta, Quaestiones disputatae, De divisione philosophiae, De Unitate intellectus, De Mente, De Intellectu et Intelligigili,*—it is in works of this sort, as well as in the many commentaries on Aristotle that we find developed discussions of the nature of knowledge. In the 17th-19th centuries we find such significant title terms as the following: The *Novum organum* of Francis Bacon, the *Discours de la méthode* and the *Meditationes de prima philosophia* with René Descartes; with Kant, the term *Kritik* becomes synonymous with the theory of knowledge; then such expressions as *Erkenntnis-theorie, Erkenntnislehre, Gnosiologia, Critica, Creteriologia* and *Epistemologia* made their appearance. Among the Thomists, the expressions *Réalisme critique* (or *méthodique, naturel, métaphysique*) designates, according to the intentions of the authors who make use of it, a treatise in epistemology. For the history of the evolution of these terms and notions, cf. Régis, L. M., *La critique néo-Thomiste est-elle Thomiste?* ed. cit., pp. 106-125; Eisler, R., *Wörterbuch . . . .*, ed cit., vol. I, pp. 371-395, 356, 500-501, 579, 877; vol. III, pp. 331-334, 395-406, 617-626; Baldwin, J. M., *Dictionary of Philosophy and Psychology,* ed. cit., vol. I, p. 333, 414. In the present study, the term epistemology is understood in its English meaning, and covers all the problems dealing with human knowledge; I am not using the term in the very restricted sense given to it by the school of Louvain (cf. Van Steenberghen, Msgr. F., *Epistémologie* (Louvain, 1945) pp. 10-18.

3.   For the history of this increasing fascination exercised by Idealism upon neo-Thomism, cf. Regis, L. M., *Ibid.,* pp. 126-144.

4.   Cf. Noël, Msgr. L., *Le Réalisme immédiat,* (Louvain, 1938) pp. 27-29, 45-48, 97-117, 134-138, 283, 285; Roland-Gosselin, M.D., *Essai d'une étude critique de la connaissance,* ed. cit., pp. 10-11, Maréchal, J., *Le point de départ de la Métaphysique,* ed. cit., pp. 38-40.

5.   Cf. *Descartes à l'abbé de Launay,* Correspondances, CCXLIX, ed. cit., vol. III, p. 420; *Quintae responsiones,* ed. cit., vol. VII, p. 356; *Sextae responsiones,* ibid., pp. 440-441. This opinion had quite a vogue and can be found in the writings of a great many modern thinkers. Cf. Brunschvicg, L., *Les âges de l'intelligence* (Paris, Alcan, 1937) pp. 14, 20, 62, 67, 83, 132; Meyerson, E., *Le cheminement de la pensée* (Paris, Alcan, 1931) paragraphe 429, pp. 676-677; *Essais* (Paris, Vrin, 1936) p. 54; Dewey, J., *Logic. The Theory of Inquiry,* (New York, Holt, 1938) p. 97.

6.   The term epistemology is not found in Descartes. It is, in fact, of relatively recent date: it was used for the first time, in the middle of the 19th century by J. F. Ferrier. (Cf. Eisler, R.,

Wörterbuch, ed. cit., vol. I, p. 356.) The expression used by Descartes is *Discours de la méthode.* Cf. *Oeuvres complètes,* ed. cit., vol. VI, pp. 1-78.

7. While it is true that Descartes admits the classical definition of science as certain and evident knowledge (Cf. *Regulae,* II, ed. cit., vol. X, pp. 362-363), yet he does not admit that a knowledge which is evident for one can be inevident for another. Hence he excludes all possibility of discussion and disputes concerning an evident truth. Only the probable, which in the speculative order is synonymous with error, is open to discussion (Cf. *Discours de la méthode,* vol. VI, pp. 8,, 18, 31) ; hence his total condemnation of scholastic philosophy because of the perpetual discussions that it contains. (Cf. *Discours,* vol. VI, p. 8, ll. 21-22, ed. cit.).

8. Cf. *Regulae,* II, ed. cit., vol. X,p. 363; *Discours,* p. 19, 1. 22; *Correspondence,* DXIV, vol. V, pp. 176-177; *Discours,* p. 11, ll. 24-25.

9. Cf. *Discours,* p. 18, 1. 17, ed. cit., vol. VI; *Regulae,* III, vol. X, pp. 367-369; *Regulae,* IV, vol. X, pp. 372-373; *Regulae,* II, vol. X, p. 362. For the relations between the *evidence,* the *clearness* and the *distinction* of ideas in Descartes, cf. Gilson, E., *Discours de la Méthode,* Texte et Commentaire (Paris, Vrin, 1925) pp. 200-204.

10. "Sed quotiescumque duorum de eadem re judicia in contrarias partes feruntur, certum est alterum saltem decipi, ac ne unus quidem videtur habere scientiam: si enim hujus ratio esset certa

et evidens, ita illam alteri posset proponere, ut ejus etiam intellectum tandem convinceret." *Regulae*, II, vol. X, p. 363.

11.   Cf. *Discours*, p. 33, 11. 9-12; *Principia philosophiae*, I, 60, vol. VIII, pp. 28-29; *Regulae*, III, vol. X, pp. 369-370; *Regulae*, IV, pp. 372-373; *Regulae*, II, p. 362.

12.   Cf. *Discours*, p. 18, 11. 16-23; *Regulae*, II, vol. X, p. 362: Omnis scientia est cognito certa et evidens; neque doctior est qui de multis dubitat, quam qui de iisdem numquam cogitavit..... Atque ita per hanc propositionem rejicimus illas omnes probabiles tantum cognitiones, nec nisi perfecte cognitis, et de quibus dubitari non potest, statuimus esse credendum."

13.   Cf. *Regulae*, II, vol. X, pp. 362-364; *Discours*, p. 8, 1. 29. For the use of the *probable* in the practical order and its exclusion from the speculative thought, cf. Gilson, E., *Discours de la Méthode*, Texte et Commentaire, pp. 195, 231-234, 245, 358-359.

14.   Cf. *Discours*, p. 6, 11. 8-9; p. 8, 1. 18 -p. 9, 1. 2; *Regulae*, II, vol. X ,pp. 362-363; *Epistola ad G. Voethium*. Pars prima, vol. VIII, p. 26: "Philosophia autem illa vulgaris quae in scholis et Academiis docetur, est tantum congeries quaedam opinionum, maxima ex parte dubitarum, ut ex continuis disputationibus, quibus exagitari solent, apparet; atque inutilium, ut longa experientia jam docuit: nemo enim unquam ex materia prima, formis substantialibus, qualitatibus occultis, et

talibus, aliquid in usum suum convertit. Qua propter nullo modo rationi consentaneum est, ut ii qui opiones istas, quas ipsimet fatentur esse incertas, didicerunt, alios odio habeant, quia certiores invenire conantur." Cf. also, *Regulae*, I, vol. X, p. 360-361; *Principes de la Philosophie*, Préface, vol. IX, p. 14; *Traité de la Lumière*, vol. XI, pp. 1-36; *Traité de l'homme*, vol. XI, pp. 201-202.

15. Cf. *Discours*, p. 18, 11. 16-18; p. 19, 11. 27-29; p. 21, 11. 18-24; p. 33, 1. 20; *Meditationes de prima philosophia*, Med. III, vol. VII, pp. 35-36. For the distinction between evidence as used in the *Discours de la méthode* to grasp truth and evidence as used in metaphysics to discover truth, cf. Gilson, E., *loc. cit.*, pp. 312-314, 360-362.

16. The criticism of scholastic philosophy and of the sources of its errors appears constantly in Descartes. Cf. especially the following passages: *Discours*, p. 8, 11. 18 -p. 9, 1. 2; p. 18, 11. 18-21; *Principia philosophiae*, I, vol. VIII, pp. 35-38; *Meditatio* VI, vol. VII, p. 82-83; *Le Monde*, vol. XI, chap. I, pp.3-6 chap II, pp. 7-14; chap. V, pp. 25-26; chap. VII, 41-48,. For the whole question of the arguments advanced by Descartes against sensation as the starting point of scholastic philosophy, cf. Gilson, E., *loc. cit.*, pp. 308-312, 358, 367-369.

17. Cf. *Discours*, p. 17, 11. 14-26. *Regulae*, II, vol. X, pp. 363-364, p. 365; *Regulae*, III, vol. X, p. 368; *Regulae*, IV, vol. X, pp. 372-373; *Regulae*, X, pp. 405-406; *Regulae*, XIV, pp. 439-440;

Correspondence, CCXXXIII, *A Mersenne,* vol. III, pp. 339-340; DXIV, *A Burman,* vol. V, p. 175; cf. Gilson, E., *loc. cit.,* pp. 180-187.

18.   Cf. *Discours,* p. 17, 1. 27- p 18, 1. 8; *Regulae,* IV, vol. X, pp. 371-379. On *analysis* as a method for the discovery of truth, its mathematical origin, and its various applications in Descartes, cf. Gilson, E., *loc. cit.,* pp. 187-195.

19.   Cf. *Discours,* p. 18, 1. 12; *Regulae,* IV, vol. X, p. 372, 1. 11: "At si methodus recte explicet quomodo mentis intuitu sit utendum, ne in errorem vero contrarium delabamur, et quomodo deductiones inveniendae sint, ut ad omnium cognitionem perveniamus: nihil aliud requiri mihi videtur, ut sit completa, cum nullam scientiam haberi posse, nisi per mentis intuitu vel deductionem, jam ante dictum sit. Neque enim illa extendi potest ad docendum quomodo ipsae operationes faciendae sint, quia sunt omnium simplicissimae et primae, adeo ut, nisi illis uti jam ante posset intellectus noster, nulla ipsius methodi praecepta quantumcumque facilia comprehenderet. Aliae autem regulae, quarum auxilio mentis operationes dirigere se contendit Dialectica (i.e. the Logic of the ancients), hic sunt inutiles, vel potius inter impedimenta numerandae, quia nihil puro rationis lumini superaddi potest, quod illud aliquo modo non obscuret."

20.   Cf. *Discours,* p. 18, 11. 18-20; p. 37, 11. 4-30; *Meditationes de Prima philosophia,* Med. II, vol. VII, pp. 82-83; *Principia philosophiae,* I, vol. VIII, pp. 35-38.

21. Cf. *Discours,* p. 31, 1. 27 - p. 33, 1. 20; *Principia philosophiae,* I, vol. VIII, pp. 6-7; *Meditationes de prima philosophia,* Med. II, vol. VII, p. 25; *Regulae,* XII, vol. X, p. 421; XIV, vol. X, p. 432; for an account of an historical antecedent of the Cartesian cogito as well as of its metaphysical meaning, cf. Gilson, E., *loc. cit.,* pp. 292-301; 312-314; Gouhier, H., *Essais sur Descartes* (Paris, Vrin, 1937) chap. III, pp. 107-141.

22. It is impossible to justify such large affirmations within the limits of a lecture. The reader will find in Gilson, *The Unity of Philosophical Experience,* chs. VI, VII and VIII (New York, Scribner's, 1941) pp. 152-220, the texts justifying this affirmation as well as the historical and doctrinal reasons of such a strange offspring of Cartesian spiritualism.

23. Cf. Brochard, V., *Etudes de Philosophie ancienne et moderne, Le Dieu de Spinoza,* (Paris, Alcan, 1912), pp. 332-370; cf. *Spinoza opera* (ed. Carl Gebhart, Heidelberg, 1923-1924), 4 vols., vol. I, *Court Traité,* pp. 31 ff ;vol. IV, *Epist.,* p. 7, p. 278; cf. Malebranche N., *Oeuvres complètes* (Paris, 1712) vol. I, *Entretiens sur la Métaphysique et la Religion,* p. 33, 47-54; *Recueil,* pp. 173, 269-270; vol. IX, *Méditations chrétiennes,* 9 and 10; cf. Berkeley, G., *The Works of . . . ,* (Ed. by Alex. Campbell Fraser, Oxford, 1901) 4 vols., vol. I, *Commonplace Book,* pp. 7, 92; *A Treatise concerning human knowledge,* pp. 259-295; G. G. Leibnitii, *Opera omnia* (studio Lud. Dutens, Genevae, 1768) 6 vols., vol. IV, *Discours de Métaphysique,* pp. 427-437; *Monadologie,* vol. VI, pp.

607- 623; *Essais de Théodicée,* pp. 517-571; Hume, D., *A treatise of Human Nature,* Bk. I, Parts III and IV.

24. Cf *Critique of Pure Reason,* Preface to the First Edition (1781), ed. cit., pp. 8-11. Cf. also *Ibid.,* Preface to the Second Edition, pp. 17-21; *Transcendental Analytic,* Bk. II, chap. II, pp. 188-256.

25. Cf. *Ibid., Preface to the Second Edition,* pp. 21-26; Introduction, pp. 41-48.

26. Cf. *Ibid.,* Introduction, pp. 55-62; *Transcendental Doctrine of Elements,* para. 7-8, pp. 79-91; *Transcendental Logic,* Introduction, pp. 92-101; *Transcendental Analytic,* para. 10, pp. 111-115; para. 13-17, pp. 120-257.

27. Cf. *Transcendental Analytic,* para. 20 ff., pp. 160-175. It is at this point that, for an understanding of Kant, we must distinguish between the datum which is purely empirical and enters our consciousness through intuition, and the phenomenon which is the datum plus the a priori form of the faculty in which the datum is received. These two elements, the datum and the phenomenon, are incapable, according to Kant, of constituting an object (cf. *Transcendental Aesthetic),* para. 1-7, pp. 65-72. That is why a third element is needed for the constitution of the object as such. This element is a category, which is a formal condition supra-sensible or universal, or a pure concept of the understanding (cf. *Ibid.,* para. 8, pp. 82-91). It is in this same place that Kant distinguishes between a priori and transcen-

dental knowledge (cf. *Ibid.*, Introduction, II, p. 95) : the first is related to objects of sensible experience, while the second is concerned with the laws of thought (cf. *Ibid.*, pp. 95-97). For Kant's own definition of his critical vocabulary, cf. *Transcendental Dialectic*, Bk. I, section 1, pp. 309-314.

28. The a priori of sensibility (Space and Time) and the a priori of understanding (the categories) are Kantian concepts; they are the forms of phenomena (cf. *Transcendental Aesthetic*, para. 128, pp. 65-91; *Transcendental Logic*, Introduction, I-II pp. 92-97) ; what he is concerned with here, is the question of pure concepts or forms of thought which are related to acts of pure thought and not to a particular content.

29. Cf. the celebrated division of Logic into Analytic and Dialectic (*Transcendental Logic*, Introduction, III, pp. 97-99). This division is not identical with the Greek division of logic in analytics and topics, because probability also belongs to the domain of Analytics. Cf. *Transcendental Dialectic*, Introduction, I, 297. It is a division between a logic of truth and a logic of illusion (*Ibid.*, pp. 296-301).

30. Cf. *Transcendental Analytic*, Bk. I, para. 22-23, pp. 161-164; para. 27, pp. 173-175; *Transcendental Dialectic*, Introduction, II, pp. 300-307.

31. Cf. *Transcendental Analytic*, Bk. I, para. 26, pp. 170-173; Bk. II, ch. 2, pp. 188-256.

32. Cf. *ibid.,* ch. 3, pp. 256-275, especially 262-263.

33. Cf. *ibid.,* ch. 3, pp. 264-265; *Transcendental Dialectic,* Introduction, I and II, pp. 297-307.

34. Cf. *Transcendental Dialectic,* Bk. II, ch. 1, pp. 328-383; cf. also Introduction, I, p. 297; Bk. I, section 2, pp. 315-321; Bk. II, ch. 3, section 1, pp. 485-486; section 6, pp. 514-521; *Transcendental Doctrine of Method,* ch. 1, pp. 574-628. Yet Kant admits a practical finalization of this transcendental illusion to be found in the speculative order, namely moral action (cf. *ibid.,* ch. 2, pp. 629-652). His conclusions is that this negative role of the transcendental dialectic coincides with the data of common sense: "in matters which concern all men without distinction nature is not guilty of any partial distribution of her gifts, and that in regard to the essential ends of human nature the highest philosophy cannot advance further than it is possible under the guidance which nature has bestowed even upon the most ordinary understanding." (p. 652).

35. "Thus regarded philosophy is a mere idea of a possible science which nowhere exists in concreto but to which, by many different paths we endeavour to approximate, until the one true path, overgrown by the products of sensibility, has at last been discovered . . . . . Till then we cannot learn philosophy; for where it is, who is in possession of it, and how shall we recognize it? We can only learn to philosophize, that is, to exercise the talent of reason, in accordance with

its universal principles, on certain actually existing attempts at philosophy, always, however, reserving the right of reason to investigate, to confirm or to reject these principles in their very sources" *Transcendental Doctrine of Method,* ch. 3, p. 657).

36.   *Transcendental Aesthetic,* para. 8, p. 91. It is evidently impossible to undertake here a point by point refutation of Kant (always supposing that a refutation of this sort is possible). The only thing that we can do is to indicate the inconsistencies of his position. Thus Kant accepts the object as phenomenon as the initial postulate of his critical undertaking. Now the object-phenomenon necessarily implies, as Kant himself acknowledges, the postula of the noumenon or of the *ding ansich.* But if the one is real and knowable, why not the other? The reason is that Kant, in spite of his efforts, remained under the influence of the metaphysics of Christian Wolff, a metaphysics of the possible as opposed to the actual, of the intelligible as opposed to being; and since the proofs brought forward by Wolff are verbal rather than metaphysical, they could not satisfy a man of Kant's intellectual stature. That is why Kant came to the conclusion that it was illegitimate to go from the rational to the existential, because the rational is the form of our thought and not that of things.

37.   Cf. *Transcendental Dialectic,* Bk. II, ch. 1 and 2, pp. 328-484.

38.   For the different meanings of the words *naïve* and *critical,* cf. Eisler, R., Wörterbuch . . ., *ed cit.,*

under *Realismus,* vol. II, pp. 622-632; Régis, L. M., loc. cit., pp. 111-114, 178-182.

39. "Il n'y a pas de bonne métaphysique sans pro-légomènes critiques, et Kant, et avant lui, Descartes, ont appris pour toujours à la philosophie quelque chose qui constitue un progrès essentiel de la pensée humaine" (Noël, L., *Le Réalisme immédiat* (Louvain, 1938) pp. 23-24). "La pensée n'est donc pas simplement, pour une philosophie systématique, un point de départ possible parmi bien d'autres. C'est nous paraît-il, le seul point de depart légitime." *(Ibid.,* pp. 28 and 45-46, 102).

40. ". . . . la métaphysique ne sera suffisamment assurée sans une étude préliminaire de la connaissance, ni la théorie de la connaissance achevée sans une métaphysique, à supposer que celle-ci soit possible. . . . Dés lors, le problème critique accepté prend une valeur logique antérieure à toute métaphysique, puisqu'il s'interroge sur la possibilité de la science et de la métaphysique. Il ne doit pas avoir recours à cette derniere pour établir la solution qu'il cherche, tant du moins que n'aura pas été justifiée la valeur de la connaissance et montrée la nécessité, pour connaître l'esprit lui-même, d'une science de l'être (Roland-Gosselin, M. D., *Essai d'une Etude critique de la connaissance,* Introduction, ed. cit., pp. 10-11).

41. Cf. *Le point de départ de la métaphysique,* ed. cit., pp. 8, 12-32. Cf. also Van Steenberghen, Msgr. F., *Epistémologie,* ed. cit., pp. 34-39.

42. Cf. Maréchal, *loc. cit.*, Bk. II, p. 34. For the studies on neo-Thomistic epistemologies in relation to Thomism, cf. supra, note 1, c, p. 61.

43. *Notes d'Epistémologie thomiste*, ed. cit., p. 23.

44. *Le Réalisme immédiat*, ed. cit., pp. 23-24.

45. *Ibid.*, pp. 45-46.

46. *Ibid.*, pp. 28, 45-46, 102.

47. *Ibid.*, pp. 23, 26, 29, 103, 114, 138. For the meaning of the word postulate, cf. Eisler, *loc. cit.*, vol. II, pp. 477-479.

48. *Le Réalisme immédiat*, pp. 97-101; cf. Picard, G., *Le problème critique fondamental*, ed. cit., pp. 1, 19-20, 76-79.

49. *Le Réalisme immédiat*, p. 108: "Il est un passage célèbre qui semble, du fond du moyen âge, faire écho à la critique moderne . . . Revenant sur son acte à la réflexion, l'esprit se rend compte de la proportion qu'il y a entre son acte et les choses. Comment ne pas reconnaître ici la réflexion critique dont nous parlions tantôt? . . . c'est bien le Cogito, et c'est le point de départ de la critique."

50. Cf. *Le Réalisme immédiat*, pp. 90, 260, 270; Maréchal, J., *Ibid.*, pp. 38-40; Van Steenberghen, Msgr. F., *Epistémologie*, p. 58; Roland-Gosselin, M.D., *Essai*, pp. 14-18.

51. Cf. *Le Réalisme immédiat*, pp. 98, 101, 273; *Notes d'Epistémologie*, p. 141.

52.   Cf. *Le réalisme immédiat,* pp. 90, 114, 166-170,
       260-262, 270-273, 283.

53.   Cf. *Ibid.,* p. 23.

54.   Cf. *Ibid.,* p. 90.

55.   Cf. Régis, L. M., *loc. cit.,* pp. 161-178. These
       pages contain the history of the transformations
       which Msgr. Noël has imposed on these Thomistic
       notions in order to give them a Cartesian critical
       function.

56.   On the division of logic according to Saint
       Thomas, cf. *In Post. Anal.,* Bk. I, lect. I, nn. 5-7,
       (Leonine edition). In these texts the certitude and
       evidence of *scientia* are opposed *toto caelo* to a
       knowledge which is probable or dialectical. In
       this Saint Thomas does no more than reaffirm
       Aristotelian doctrine. Cf. Régis, L. M., *L'Opinion
       selon Aristote,* Paris, Vrin, 1935, pp. 81-108
       (the probable and appearance) ; pp. 185-203 (the
       probable and certitude).

57.   No adversary of Thomism contests the fact that
       common sense is realistic, that it literally places
       us in contact with a substantial world, and that
       the sort of knowledge it gives is rooted in the reali-
       ties with which we are called upon to deal in
       every day life. Some go even further than this
       and admit that common sense is the necessary point
       of departure for all scientific explanation: "Le
       monde du sens commun, si mal coordonné qu'il
       soit, constitue néanmoins le point de départ de
       toutes nos tentatives d'explication." Meyerson, E.,

Essais, (Paris, Vrin, 1937), p. 55. The same author has also said: "Le physician, qui part du sens commun, ne peut se passer d'une ontologie, tout le long de ses travaux et de ses raisonnements, et cette ontologie ne saurait, par ses fondements, différer de nature de celle de la perecption immédiate, ainsi que nous y avons maintes fois insisté" *(Ibid.,* p. 68). But what the adversaries of Thomism do not admit is that common sense is *scientifically* realistic; and they are perfectly right if the word *science* is taken in its modern meaning. And that is why the same E. Meyerson who has so strongly affirmed the absolute necessity of common sense for the very existence of science, has always opposed those who have tried to interpret his works realistically, that is to say, as establishing scientifically the realism of human knowledge. His last writings *(Essais,* pp. 59-105, 170-186) are an official admission that he is a partisan of the "Geisteswissenschaften" and not of the "Naturwissenschaften." For the meaning of these two words, within the limits of epistemology, cf. Eisler, R., *Wörterbuch* . . ., under "Wissenschaft," vol. III, pp. 617-625, where is to be found the history of the separation between "Naturwissenschaften" and "Geisteswissenschaften" by Steinthal, Helmholtz, Dilthey, Wundt, etc. If therefore by a pre-philosophical epistemology it is possible to show that common sense is realistic, such a demonstration is one that everybody admits, including the most idealistic philosophers. But this leaves unestablished, scientifically as well as philosophically, the further proposition that this realism is critical, which is precisely what the neo-Thomists want to prove.

58. In Thomism, it is not the realism of common sense which *founds* philosophical realism, but, on the contrary, it is philosophical realism which explains the realistic instinct of common sense and manifests the solidity of its foundations and its limits. In Thomism, it is metaphysics which gives to logic its principles, that is to say, the radical distinction between truth and error; it is not logic that teaches metaphysics what being and non-being are: "Philosophus enim *primus* debet disputare contra negantes principia singularium scientiarum, quia omnia principia firmantur super hoc principium quod affirmatio et negatio non sunt simul vera. Illa autem sunt propriissima hujus scientiae, cum *sequantur rationem entis,* quod est hujus philosophiae primum subjectum. Verum autem et falsum pertinet proprie ad considerationem *logici* . . . nam verum et falsum sunt in mente. Ad errorem autem qui accidit circa *esse et non esse sequitur* error circa verum et falsum: nam per esse et non esse verum et falsum definitur." *(IV Metaph.,* lect 17, n. 736 ed. Marietti). Now the whole neo-Scholastic epistemological problem consists precisely in establishing that the knowledge of common sense is true, that is to say ,that it has a *certain being* as its object. But it belongs to metaphysics to define Being as being and its diverse modes: and that is why it belongs to metaphysics to establish the realism of common sense, and not to common sense to establish realism of metaphysical

knowing (cf. *Summa Theologiae,* I-II, q. 66, a. 5, ad 4).

59.   Cf. Reid, Th., *The Inquiry into the Human Mind on the Principle of Common Sense,* (London, 1853) ; *The Essays on the Intellectual Powers of Man,* Essay II, ch. 2; Garrigou-Lagrange, R., *Le Sens commun, La philosophie de l'être et les formules dogmatiques,* (Paris, Desclée De Brouwer, 1936, 4th ed.,) Part 1, "Ce qu'est le sens commun," pp. 15-153. This last work contains such statements as the following: "Nous serons amenés à conclure que le sens commun est, *à l'état rudi-*mentaire, non pas *une* philosophie mais *la* philosophie" (p. 79) ; "Le sens commun serait donc la solution confuse mais certaine et strictement suffisante au commun des hommes, des principales questions métaphysiques, morales et religieuses: qu'est-ce que l'être, le vrai, le bien, le beau? . . . Dieu est-il, qu'est-il en lui-même et pour nous? . . . (p. 81) Cf. the pertinent criticism which M. Gilson has made of this pseudo-Scholastic notion (which, in fact has its origin in Reid), in *Réalisme Thomiste et critique de la connaissance* (Paris, Vrin, 1939), pp. 18-40. It is a constant Thomistic doctrine that a power is not specified in the same way as is a habit or a virtue (cf. *In III Sent.,* dist. 33, q. 1, a. 1, sol. 1a; *Summa Theologica,* q. 79, a. 9; *In II Sent.,* dist. 24, q. 2, a. 11). Hence the proof of the realism of the intellect as a power is not identical with a proof of the realism of this or that habit. Now common sense is neither intellect as a power nor intellect as a habit; still less is it the habit of wisdom, even in an inchoative

state. But, in that case, what is the function of common sense realism as a foundation of metaphysical realism? If common sense consisted in the use of our intellect as a power, then, since the intellect is infallible in the presence of its proper object, no common sense truth could be denied by anyone, which is certainly not the case. The same argument holds if common sense were considered to be an intellectual virtue, for such a virtue is "quo infallibiliter verum dicatur" *(Quaest. disp. De Veritate* q. 15, a. 7, c.; q. 14, a. 9, c; *In III Sent.,* dist. 23, q. 1, a. 4, sol. Ia; *In VI Ethic. Nic.,* lect. III.)

60. "Ens primum cognitum" is the object of our intellect as a power, while "ens in quantum ens" is the proper object of the most perfect of our acquired habits, wisdom. The first coincides with our very first intellectual activity, which is a condition of imperfection, while the second is the home of the intellect in search of its proper perfection and already possessing it in part. These are quite elementary notions in Thomism, and it is rather surprising that a thinker such as Msgr. Van Steenberghen, who admits to a long association with the thought of Saint Thomas *(Epistémologie,* p. 7), nevertheless holds that the analogical concept of being, which is "ens in quantum ens," is "le fruit d'une experience quelconque et qu'il ne peut y avoir pour l'être d'experience privilégiée" *(Ibid.,* p. 154, note 1, and p. 212). The experience of the "ens primum cognitum" is universal in the sense that it belongs to all human beings; but the experience of "ens in quantum ens" is an intel-

lectual wealth proper to the philosopher, for it is necessary to have a great maturity of mind in order to possess it (cf. *Summa contra Gentes,* III, cap. 48). It is known too, that metaphysics is situated at the top of the ladder of knowing (cf. *In VI Eth. Nic.,* lect. VII, n. 1211), since it is concerned with God and the divine things, objects which men are much too inclined to neglect (cf. *Summa contra Gentes,* I cap. 4).

61.   Cf. *In Post. An.,* Bk II, lect. XX; *Summa Theologiae,* I-II q. 51, a. 1; q. 63, a. 1;*Quaest. disp. De Veritate,* q. 16, a. 1, c; According to Saint Thomas, "ens primum cognitum" is neither being as being nor thought, not God, but sensible and concrete being; "Dicendum quod objectum intellectus est quoddam commune, scilicet ens et verum, sub quo comprehenditur etiam ipse actus intelligendi. Unde intellectus potest suum actum intelligere. *Sed non primo; quia nec primum objectum intellectus nostri secundum praesentem statum est quodlibet ens et verum; sed ens et verum consideratum in rebus materialibus . . .* ex quibus in cognitionem omnium aliorum devenit" *(Summa Theologiae,* I, q. 87, a. 3, ad 1).

62.   An elaborate synthesis of such a neo-Scholastic epistemology can be found in the recently published volume of Msgr. Fernand Van Steenberghen, *Epistémologie,* (Louvain, 1945). This book is divided into three parts: an *analytical* part, a *critical* part, and a *logic* (cf. p. 222). Here are some of the conclusions which the author has reached: "Le problème épistémologique est le problème

philosophique *fondamental* une philosophie systématique *doit* s'ouvrir par l'examen de ce problème parce qu'il conditionne tous les autres . . . 3)
L'objet primordial de l'analyse et de la critique
épistémologique doit être la connaissance du réel
ou de l'être . . . je ne puis parler du réel que dans
la mesure où je le connais: sous ce rapport, nous
pouvons et nous devons souscrire à la méthode
du *cogito* cartésien . . . (p. 211)." Here, too, are
the imperfections which he finds in the epistemology of Saint Thomas: "la perception sensible n'est
pas dûment critiquée; les caractères propres du
concept d'être ne sont pas suffisamment mis en
relief . . . ; l'exposée de la doctrine de l'abstraction
s'encombre de trop d'images; l'ordre conceptuel
n'est pas toujours nettement distingué de l'ordre
réel; enfin *l'unité de la connaissance* paraît souvent
menacée par des formules qui juxtaposent la sensation et l'intellection, l'objet sensible (individuel)
et l'objet intelligible (universel)" (p. 240). But
after an attentive reading of the *Epistémologie* of
Msgr. Van Steenberghen, I find that his notion
of sensible perception is certainly not more precise than the one proposed by Saint Thomas Aquinas
when he distinguishes between the "per se" objects
(proprium et commune) and the "per accidens"
object of sensation (cf. *In De Anima,* Bk. II, lect.
XIII) ; for this Thomistic doctrine teaches what
is infallible and what is fallible in sensible perception and the sources of this fallibility. The
pages of the *Epistémologie* devoted to this problem (pp. 170-187) contain merely what everybody
admits, including the Idealists, namely that the

data of our immediate consciousness, or the data
of common sense are realistic, and that they imply
objective qualities and quantities, and real space
and time; but this affirmation does not tell me
either the why or the how of such a state of affairs. The author's account of abstraction (pp. 111-
113, 115-121, 152-154) affirms that the concept
is an abstract and universal representation (p.
113), but it does not show, except by *examples,*
how it is so. It seems to me that the luminous
passage of Saint Thomas' commentary on the
De Trinitate of Boethius (q. 5, a. 3), is by way
of contrast a highly satisfactory explanation of the
immediate data of our consciousness. As for the
distinction between the conceptual order and the
real order, all the formulae that Saint Thomas re-
peatedly uses (the opposition between *modus rei*
and *modus cognoscendi* or *repraesentandi,* between
res and *similitudo seu species,* between *esse rei*
and *esse intelligible,* between *praedicabilia* and
praedimamenta or *intentiones* and *naturae indi-
viduales,* etc. . . .) should remove all possible am-
biguity on this point. As concerns the unity of human knowledge, it is by the causality of the human person that Saint Thomas explains it and
not by the unity of the object (cf. the following
significant texts, *In I Sent.,* 17, q. 1, a. I, c.; *In
III Sent.,* 8, a. 2, ad 3; *In III Sent.,* 17 q. 1, a. 1,
sol. 1, ad 1; *In IV Sent.,* 44, q. 1, a. 1, sol. 3, ad 3;
Quaestio disputata De Veritate, q. 2, a. 6, ad. 3;
q. 20, a. 1, ad 2; q. 22, a. 13, ad 7; q. 27; a. 3,
ad 25; *Quodlibet* 7, a. 11, ad 3; *Quodlibet* 9, a. 7,
c; *Quaest. disp. De Spiritualibus creaturis,* a. 2, ad

2; a. 10, ad 15; *In I De Anima,* lect. X, n. 152; *Quaest. disp. De Anima,* a. 19, c.; *Summa Theologiae,* I-II, q. 16, a. I, c.). Finally, it is not Saint Thomas himself who has ever been guilty of separating the sensible and the intelligible (cf. his notion of the "sensible per accidens" which is "intelligible per se," and his explanation of the formation of the universal, *In II De Anima,* lect. XIII; *In II Post. Anal.,* lect. XXI, n. 14; *De Ente et Essentia,* ch. 3). It is rather some of the disciples of Saint Thomas who have brought about the disjunction of these two elements of the human knowledge, much in the same way as some neo-Scholastics, following Descartes, have considered man to be two substances (soul and body) whose unity seems to consist in non-interference.

63. Among the early neo-Scholastics, epistemology was a part of logic, namely *logica materialis* cf. Liberatore, *Institutiones philosophicaQ,* (Prati, Giachetti, 1889) p. 23; Tongiorgi, *Institutiones philosophicae,* (Bruxellis, Goemaere, 1864) p. 18. According to Cardinal Mercier, epistemology is a part of psychology (cf. *Critériologie Générale* Paris, Alcan, 1900) Introduction, pp. II-III. In general, the school of Louvain and some Jesuit publications make of epistemology the gateway to philosophy without indicating whether it is a part of logic cf. Noël, L., *Le réalisme immédiat,* pp. 163-167, 291, et., Maréchal, J., *Le point de départ de la Métaphysique. Lecons sur le développement historique et théorique du problème de la connais-*

sance (Paris, Alcan, 1922-1926) 5 volumes, or by making logic a part of epistemology; cf. Van Steenberghen, Msgr. F., *Epistémologie* (Louvain, Institut Supérieur de Philosophie, 1945) pp. 23-24, 222. This position is identical with that of Descartes and Kant, both of whom considered the problem of knowledge as an issue to be examined before any philosophical speculation (cf. *supra*, notes 8-10, 24-30). For contemporary neo-Thomists in general, epistemology is part of metaphysics. For some, it is the first part; cf. Maritain, J., *Les Dégrés du Savoir* (Paris, Desclée De Brouwer, 1932) pp. 153-154; Garrigou-Lagrange, R., *Le Réalisme du principe de finalité* (Paris, Desclée De Brouwer, 1932) pp. 149 ff., pp. 256, 160; for others it is the second part; cf. Pirotta "De Metaphysicae defensivae natura," in *Angelicum,* IV (1927), pp. 252-270; Gredt, *Elementa philosophiae* (Freiburg in B., 1929) vol. II, nn. 658 ff.; some consider it to be the terminus of all metaphysical speculation because it is a sort of reflexive metaphysics; cf. Jolivet, R., *Le Thomisme et la critique de la connaissance* (Paris, Desclée De Brouwer, 1933) p. 110, or bcause it is a metaphysics that is always aware of its proper work and goal; cf. Gilson, E., *Le Realisme méthodique* (Paris, Tequi) p. 86.

64. *Metaph.,* Bk. I, ch. 2, 982 a. 18. Cf. also the admirable definition and division of all human knowing on the basis of the notion of order in *In I Eth. Nic.,* lect. I, nn. 1-2.

65. This opposition of kinds of knowing which confront our consciousness as true in spite of their opposition is the true epistemological problem. It is the problem which rouses in us the *admiratio* and *dubitatio* or *quaestio* which lie at the beginning of philosophical reflexion (cf. *In I Metaph.*, lect. III, nn. 54-56); the Cartesian doubt, which dealt with the truths of common sense, and the Kantian doubt, which dealt with the validity of the existence of noumena, are no more than consequences of this problem; in fact, they are consequences which result from a metaphysical postulate as to the nature of the real.

66. Cf. the exposition of the Cartesian and Kantian epistemologies given above.

67. The notion of order requires three elements: 1) a relation of priority and posteriority; 2) a distinction of the realities ordered; 3) unity within the distinction (cf. *Summa Theologiae,* II-II q. 26, a. 1, c.; *In XII Metaph.*, lect. XII, especially n. 2637; *Summa Theologiae,* I, q. 11, a 3, c.). This means that multitude is the matter of which order is the form: "non invenitur una forma in pluribus suppositis nisi unitate ordinis ut forma multitudinis ordinate" (*Summa Theologiae,* q. 39, a. 3, c.).

68. ". . . cujuslibet habitus cognoscitivus duo objectum habet, scilicet, *id quod* materialiter cognoscitur, quod est sicut materiale objectum, et *id per quod* cognoscitur, quod est formalis ratio objecti" (*Summa Theologiae,* II-II, q. 1, a. 1, c.).—Materi-

alis diversitas objecti non diversificat habitum sed solum formalis. Cum ergo scibile sit proprium objectum scientiae, non diversificantur scientiae secundum diversitatem materialem scibilium, sed secundum diversitatem eorum formalem" *(In I Post. An.,* lect. XLI, n. 11, cf. also lect. XX, n. 4-6). It is by basing himself on this notion of object that Saint Thomas Aquinas distinguishes three kinds of knowledge and the method proper to each; cf. *In Boethium De Trinitate,* q. 6, a. 1: "Utrum oporteat versari in naturalibus rationabiliter, in mathematicis disciplinabiliter, et in divinis intelligibiliter."

69 According to Descartes, in fact, it is the clear and distinct idea which specifies both intelligence and science, since every truth must necessarily be scientific and must proceed according to the requirements of mathematics and by reflection on thought. Furthermore the body of the sciences must be one with a strict unity (cf. *Discours,* ed. cit., pp. 11-15; *Cogitationes privatae,* ed. cit., vol. X, p. 215; *Préface aux Principes de la Philosophie,* ed. cit., vol. IX, p. 14); and contrary to the scholastics who do not place any connection among the sciences but only among the moral virtues (cf. *Summa Theologiae,* I-II, q. 65, a. 1, ad 3), Descartes rejects this specification by objects and proclaims a connection ". . . cum *scientiae omnes* nihil aliud sint quam humana sapientia *quae semper una et eadem manet,* quantumvis differentibus subjectis applicata . . ." *Regulae,* I, ed. cit., vol. X, p. 360, and p. 361). For the difference between the specification of a

power and the specification of the habits of the
same power, cf. *In III Sent.*, 33, q. 1, a. 1, sol. 1;
In II Sent., 24, q. 2, a. 2; *Summa Theologiae*,
I, q. 79, a. 9, c.).

70. The Kantian *a priori*, which defines the knowing
subjectively, makes of our powers of knowledge
not efficient but formal causes of knowing. Sensible data, being essentially unstable are the matter
of knowledge, while our powers are the form
(cf. *Critique of Pure Reason*, Introduction, ed.
cit., pp. 41-45; *Transcendental Aesthetic*, Para. 1,
p. 65; para. 3, p. 70; para. 6, pp. 76-78; para. 8,
pp. 82-91; *Transcendental Dialectic*, Introduction,
pp. 297-307.

71. For the notion of truth in Descartes, cf. Gilson,
E., *Discours de la Méthode*, ed. cit., pp. 310-320,
362-365. The notion of truth in Kant likewise belongs to the order of relation, but it is the relation
of knowledge with its object, not with the content of this object but with its form, i.e. thought:
"The nominal definition of truth, that is the agreement of knowledge with its object, is assumed as
granted . . . If truth consists in the agreement of
knowledge with its object, that object must thereby
be distinguished from other objects; for knowledge is false, if it does not agree with the object
to which it is related even although it contains
something which may be valid of other objects.
Now, a general criterion of truth must be such
as would be valid in each and every instance of
knowledge, however their objects may vary. It is
obvious, however, that such a criterion—being gen-

eral—cannot take account of the varying content of knowledge (relation to its specific object).
But since truth concerns just this very content, it
is quite impossible, and indeed absurd, to ask
for a general test of the truth of such a content . . .
Since we have already entitled the content of
knowledge its matter, we must be prepared to
recognize that of the truth of knowledge, so far
as its matter is concerned, no general criterion
can be demanded. Such a criterion would by its
very nature be self-contradictory. But, on the
other hand, as regards knowledge in respect of
its mere form (leaving aside all content), it is
evident that logic, in so far as it expounds the
universal and necessary rules of the understanding, must in these rules furnish criteria of truth
. . . These criteria, however, concern only the
form of truth, that is of thought in general"
(*Transcendental Logic,* Introduction, III, pp. 97-
98). The Kantian criterion of truth is therefore
purely formal and negative and cannot enable us
to know whether we are actually in truth or in
error, since its effect is to make us know, not that
which is, i.e. the datum, but solely the laws of
the *a priori.*

72. For the nature of relation and the necessity of
the coexistence of two terms, cf. *Summa Theologiae,* I, q. 28, a. 2; *Quaest. disp. De Potentia,*
q. 7, a. 9, ad 7; *In I Sent.,* 19, q. 5, a. 1 and 2;
V Metaph., lect. XVII; *In X Metaph.,* lect. VII,
nn. 2087-2095: this last text and that of the
Summa are particularly important for the notion
of truth.

73. It would be necessary to discuss at this point this neo-Scholastic notion of a *critique* of knowledge which is to be distinguished from an *ontology* of knowledge (cf. Noël, L., *Le Réalisme immédiat,* pp. 162-167; Maréchal, *loc. cit.*, Cahier V, pp. 11-33; Van Steenberghen, *Epistémologie,* pp. 226-228). There is a surprising antinomy that we find among some neo-Scholastics concerning epistemology, namely that it was established in order to modernize Thomism, that is to say, to enable it to be a rival of Idealism. Hence epistemology is presented by them as a progress over the ancient method of philosophizing — a progress which they had learned from Descartes and Kant. Now this progress consists precisely in the distinction between the *critique* of knowledge and the *ontology* of knowledge. From this we might have been led to think that it was Idealism which distinguished these two ways of dealing with knowledge. But it does not seem that such is the case, since if it is true that Saint Thomas Aquinas "lorsqu'il traite de la connaissance, laisse presque toujours dans l'ombre les problems épistémologiques au profit des problèmes ontologiques" (pp. 35-36), the same thing is true of Kant who "ne distingue pas les problémes épistémologiques des problèmes ontologiques" (47). The school of Louvain therefore seems to be, along with Descartes, the sole representative of this distinction. It is understandable that Descartes himself should have thought it necessary to have a critique of the immediate data of common sense, since its starting point was a mathematical evidence from which

the world of qualities and substances is excluded. But it is much more surprising that a Thomist who begins with a concrete experience of a world of natures should be obliged to distinguish these two problems; for to know is to be another considered as other, and if epistemology is not the ontology of knowledge it is not exactly clear as to what it can be.

74. Cf. above, notes 64-67, where the notion of metaphysics as a vision of order, and therefore of a unified diversity is explained.

75. It is after having defined man as a thinking substance, as a mind, that Descartes defines truth as one; it is after having defined man as a composite of form and matter that Aristotle and Saint Thomas explain human knowledge as the complementary activity of the soul and the body in which each element makes its own contribution to the whole (cf. Régis, L. M., *La Critique néo-thomiste est-elle thomiste*, ed. cit., pp. 188-191).

76. Cf. especially *In XII Metaph.*, lect. XII; *Summa Theologiae*, I, q. 103-105.

77. Cf. *In II Phys.*, lect. I-XI; *Summa Theologiae*, I, q. 44-49; *Quaest. disp. De Spiritualibus Creaturis*, a. 6; *Quodlibet*, 1, a. 8, ad. 3.

78. Cf. *In X Eth. Nic.*, lect. X-XI; *Summa Theologiae*, I-II, q. 1-5.

79. Cf. *Summa Theologiae*, I, q. 77, a. 1, ad 3; q. 89, a. 1, c.; cf. also above note 62 ad finem.

80   That which characterizes Thomistic epistemology and opposes it to Idealism is the division of truth into different kinds (cf. *Summa Theologiae,* I, q. 16, aa. 6-8). But the point is that the admission of the plurality of truths is a consequence of the metaphysical evidence of the multitude and diversity of beings; just as in the case of Idealism, the unity of truth is a consequence of the metaphysical evidence of the unity of being.

81. Cf. above, note 27. The notion of object belongs to the order of relation: "dicitur autem aliquid esse objectum animae secundum quod habet aliquam habitudinem ad animam" *(Quaest. disp. De Veritate,* q. 22, a. 10, c.; cf. also, *Summa Theologiae,* I, q. 77, a. 1; q. 78, a. 1; II-II, q. 1, aa. 1-3; q. 2, aa. 2 and 5, etc. . . .) Now there are two sorts of relations possible between things and the soul: "res autem ad animam invenitur habere duplicem habitudinem: nam secundum quod ipsa res est in anima *per modum animae et non per modum sui;* aliam secundum quod anima comparatur *ad rem in suo esse existentem.* Et sic objectum animae est aliquid dupliciter: uno modo in quantum natum est esse in anima, non secundum esse proprium, sed secundum modum animae, id est spiritualiter; et haec est *ratio cognoscibilis in quantum* est cognoscibile" *(Quaest. disp. De Veritate,* q. 22 a. 10, c). Such is the true object of knowledge. With this notion we are very far from the objective materialism for which Descartes blamed Thomism. And, need I add how much more flexible such a notion is when it is compared with the rigid *a priori* of Kant.

82. If in fact, according to the text cited above (note 81), the object is the thing according to its spiritual existence in the soul, there will be as many specifically distinct objects as there are receptive capacities in the soul, that is, as there are powers of knowledge. Now, there are, at least, ten different powers of knowledge in the soul according to Saint Thomas: five external senses, four internal senses and the possible intellect (cf. *Summa Theologiae,* I, q. 78, aa. 3-4; q. 79, a. 2, and parallel passages). The notion of object explains the multiplicity of truth but not the unity of knowledge; it is rather to the knowing subject, which is one, and to reality, which is also one (at least with the unity of order), that we must turn if we are to give an account of the unity of human knowledge.

83. Cf. above, note 64 for an explanation of philosophical knowing as the vision of order or of unity in multiplicity; cf. also Régis, L. M., *La Critique néothomiste est-elle thomiste,* ed. cit., pp. 183-186.

84. At this point it would be necessary to distinguish between the abstraction which gives to the philosophy of nature and to mathematics their subjects, namely *abstracto totalis* and *abstracto formalis,* and the abstraction which gives to metaphysics its unity. This involves the whole problem of univocal and analogical concepts, for abstraction is essentially a means of unification. Now the unity of the infra-metaphysical sciences is a strict unity, that is, that definition that is reached

at the term of abstraction is a definition in a strict sense (by *genus* and *differentia*), while the unity which lies at the beginning of the metaphysical knowledge is a unity *secundum quid* or a unity of order, since being is not defined strictly (nor are any of the realities that transcend matter). For an explanation of the different kinds of abstractions and the principal texts of Saint Thomas dealing with them, cf. Régis, L. M., *Quelques Apories* (on the abstraction and specification of the sciences), in *Etudes et Recherches, Philosophie,* Cahier I (Ottawa, 1936) pp. 127-156.

85. Cf. *Summa Theologiae,* I, q. 16, a. 1, and parallel passages.

86. Cf. *Quaest. disp. De Veritate,* q. 1, a. 1; *Summa Theologiae,* q. 16, a. 3: "Unumquodque autem in quantum habet de esse, in tantum est cognoscibile." Cf. also parallel passages.

87. Cf. above, note 81, the references on the notion of object.

88. For the distinction between *intellectus* and *ratio* according to Saint Thomas Aquinas, cf. Péghaire, J., *Intellectus et Ratio selon Saint Thomas d'Aquin* (Paris, Vrin, 1936), especially pp. 29-169, and pp. 281-298.

89. Cf. above, note 62. I have collected there the principal references to the texts in which Saint Thomas explains the unification of the multitude of the operations of the different powers by ref-

erence to the unity of the human person as the efficient cause of knowledge.

90.   The Angelic Doctor unifies human operation by way of the wonderful order in efficiency and finality among the different powers: cf. *Summa Theologiae,* I, q. 77, aa. 4-6. It is impossible to meditate too much upon these texts which are so profound that they inevitably escape even repeated readings unless they are undertaken with constant attention to the text and context.

91.   It is in a text of the *De Veritate* (q. 2, a. 2) that we find the true context of a human epistemology, for that context is one of finality. In this text, knowledge is presented as a remedy for the ontological poverty of every creature. This remedy permits man to become like his cause by breaking his specific limits, which make him a being among others, participating in the infinity of God. It is in this context of the imitation of God that man and his whole activity receive their ultimate explanation.

92.   God is the principal unifier of the universe, i.e. of its multiplicity, while wisdom is the principal unifier of the multiplicity of human knowledges because it is at once *intellectus* et *ratio (In VI Eth. Nic.,* lect. VI; *Summa Theologiae,* I-II, q. 57, a. 2; qu. 66, a. 5 and parallel passages), because it judges the principles and the conclusions of all the sciences, and because it judges even the indemonstrable principles. The reason for this supremacy of wisdom lies in the fact that it has

God as the end of its proper object: "Cognoscere autem rationem entis et non entis . . . et aliorum quae consequuntur ad ens, ex quibus sicut ex terminis, constituuntur principia indemonstrabilia, pertinet ad sapientiam; *quia ens commune est proprius effectus causae altissimae* scilicet Dei" *(Summa Theologiae,* I-II, q. 66, a. 5, ad 4).

93. It is necessary to give at this point the theory of *assensus* and *certitudo* according to Saint Thomas; for these notions are the basis of his whole epistemology. The limits of a lecture do not permit such an exposition; but one will find the outline of such a theory, as well as the principal Thomistic texts, in Régis, L. M., *La critique néothomiste est-elle thomiste,* pp. 191-198.

94. Cf. Bk. II, ch. 1, 993b12-15.

95. Cf. *Ibid.,* lect. I, n. 287; cf. also: *Summa Theologiae,* II-II q. 1, a. 7.

PRINTED AT THE MARQUETTE UNIVERSITY PRESS
MILWAUKEE 3, WISCONSIN